How To Survive an Inland Revenue Investigation

An Insider's Guide for Taxpayers and their Professional Advisers

John Rignell

Former HM Inspector of Taxes

Northcote House

British Library Cataloguing-in-Publication Data
A catalogue record for this book is available from the British Library

© 1992 by John Rignell

First published February, 1992
Reprinted April, 1992
Reprinted June, 1992
Reprinted September, 1992
Reprinted June, 1993

First published in 1992 by Northcote House Publishers Ltd,
Plymbridge House, Estover Road, Plymouth PL6 7PZ, United Kingdom.
Tel: Plymouth (0752) 735251. Fax: (0752) 695699. Telex: 45635.

Typeset by Kestrel Data, Exeter
Printed and bound in Great Britain by
BPCC Wheatons Ltd, Exeter

Publisher's Note

This book has been written with the general taxpayer in mind. The views expressed are the personal views of the writer and do not represent the official view of the Inland Revenue.

If legal advice or expert assistance is required, the services of a competent professional person should be sought. The publisher is not engaged in rendering a legal or other professional service, and the book is sold on that understanding.

The publisher advises that the sections of the Income and Corporation Taxes Act and Taxes Management Act and the tax case report referred to in this publication are not the authorised official versions of those sections or the tax case report, and the actual authorised official publications should be referred to for reference purposes. The copyright of those items resides in the Crown.

While every effort has been made to ensure its accuracy, no responsibility for loss occasioned to any person acting or refraining from action as a result of any material in this publication can be accepted by the publisher or author.

The Publishers wish to acknowledge with gratitude the permission granted by The Controller of Her Majesty's Stationery Office to quote from Reports of Tax Cases, Statutory Tax Law and other Crown Copyright material.

Contents

Contents

List of Tables and Figures

List of Statutes

Taxes Management Act (TMA) 1970

Preface

The idea for this book came from a perceived need for direct informed and practical guidance to taxpayers who are in difficulties with the Inland Revenue. I consider that, as a retired Inspector of Taxes, I am in an ideal position to give an 'inside' picture to taxpayers of how the Revenue functions. From my experience within the Inland Revenue I can let you see through the eyes of an Inspector of Taxes how a Revenue investigation is likely to be conducted. As a civil servant it was imbued in me that I must be impartial and dispassionate in the conduct of my duties. In that same spirit of impartiality I am happy to describe the Revenue machine and its mode of operation in carrying out its investigation procedures.

When writing this book I obviously had to bear in mind any possible objections that could be raised in relation to my undertaking to abide by the provisions of the Official Secrets Act. That Act, in its original form, is very wide-ranging and has been the subject of some criticism. It certainly imposed considerable self-discipline on me, who not being a professionally trained typist, found the possibility of facing a series of re-writes quite daunting. The book that has been written is therefore perhaps not the book that may have emerged if there had been no constraints, and I would not like anybody to believe that it is possible to disclose legally all the methods, procedures, and subterfuges, in which Inspectors of Taxes may engage in order to achieve their settlement targets. Indeed some of the actions taken by individuals may well not commend themselves to the authorities.

Taxpayers are in an extraordinarily strong position. It is they who can basically decide what evidence of their activities is produced, and how much of that evidence is preserved. Their Achilles' heel is their lack of foresight and appreciation of the long arm of chance that can conspire to focus the Revenue spotlight on their activities. It is their contempt for the system, with all its flaws, that leads to their complacency and the Revenue successes.

Taxpayers' eccentric behaviour in ignoring advice, and the real perils in which their funds and freedom may stand, has to be experienced to be believed. No doubt you have heard of the Judge who, after receiving a long explanation from Counsel, declared that he was none the wiser. Counsel's response was to the effect that, while the Judge was no wiser, he was nevertheless better informed: I can assure you that after reading my book, you will be better informed.

John Rignell
September 1991

1 The Investigation Machine

Most businesses in the UK have an uninvited and unwelcome partner – the Government. Some taxpayers have felt sufficiently strongly about the matter to claim that the income tax payable on their profits was a business expense, incurred wholly and exclusively for business purposes. Such claims have been rejected by the Courts who decided that as tax is levied on profits, computed in accordance with the Income Tax Acts, it cannot also be a deduction in arriving at those profits. The Courts' view was that income tax was the Government's share of the profits made.

The Effects of Taxation Legislation
The influence of legislation on businesses is both direct and indirect. The direct effects are well documented. The indirect effects, although equally well known, are perhaps less well documented.

In some businesses the recruitment of staff is made difficult by Government regulations requiring the deduction of tax from employees' wages under the PAYE system. The difficulties arise from competing employers who seek unfair advantages in the labour market by failing to operate the PAYE scheme correctly. Employers in some highly competitive markets face difficult options: to join in the fiddles, pay excessive wage rates, or accept poorly qualified staff.

Businesses may find it difficult to obtain orders if they are not prepared to 'uplift' invoice prices artificially or to provide completely false invoices to enable their customers to make some tax free profits. Similarly, some deals will only proceed if a cash incentive is provided to the person responsible for placing an order. In certain transactions, a businessman may consider it *essential* to 'oil the wheels' to stand any chance of success.

In some predominantly cash orientated trades you may be faced with the stark alternative of having to pay cash to get the work done, or leaving the work undone. The receipts for cash payments made may be

1

irregular and prove to be of little value when it comes to substantiating the outlay involved.

Facing the demands of employees, suppliers, customers, contractors, spouses, and partners, may create a strong desire to join those engaged in tax-free enterprises. The result can be an ill advised, *ad hoc* involvement in tax evasion. Those who have engaged in tax evasion have not been from any particular trades, professions, or vocations. Tax evasion is a classless pursuit that knows no boundaries, as the desire, if not the need, to evade tax is fairly universal.

Your Chances of being Investigated

To combat unacceptable freelance activities the Government employs the Commissioners of Inland Revenue, referred to in the Taxation Acts as 'the Board'. Under the provisions of Section 1 of the Taxes Management Act 1970 the administration of the 'Income tax, corporation tax and capital gains tax shall be under the care and management of the Commissioners of Inland Revenue . . .'. The Board in turn appoint Inspectors of Taxes who act under their direction.

The often unwelcome activities of the Inspectors of Taxes tend to isolate them, making them something of a mystery to the general public, who are pleasantly surprised by any signs of 'human' behaviour. However, the first close encounters often occur in unfavourable circumstances, when the barrier erected by the accountant between his client and the Revenue is breached by the Inspector's request to see the taxpayer in person – to explain some aspects of the accounts or returns which the Inspector feels are unsatisfactory.

Taxpayers may, in such circumstances, wonder why they have been picked upon, rather than someone else – perhaps more deserving of the Inspector's attention. The answer may lie partly in the Revenue's rather tightly stretched resources. The chance of being selected for a close in-depth review, or investigation, by the Inspector is not very great, since approximately only 2.3 per cent of the business accounts received from individuals and partnerships, and only 1 per cent of company accounts are currently expected to be taken up for investigation. The percentage levels are very small but the yields are relatively high. For example, for the year ended 31st March 1989 (per the Board's annual report) the sum netted was £276.1m. and included payments of tax lost, interest on that tax, and penalties. The taxpayers involved, in addition to that total figure, paid accountancy and legal fees. They may also have been liable to VAT, a tax which is not included in the Board's figure. Clearly, it is better not to be amongst those chosen by the Inspector for investigation.

The management organisation of tax offices has changed radically in recent years aimed at increasing the number of in-depth examinations of accounts, a move which has been substantially influenced by the Parliamentary Public Accounts Committee. Even greater emphasis is being placed on the investigation of taxpayers' accounts. Separate target figures are set nationally for the number of cases to be settled each year, both for income tax and corporation tax investigations. Those figures are then sub-divided and passed to the Regional Offices and then on to Group Controllers within the Regions, who are responsible for the district offices within their groups. Finally, targets are allocated to the individual districts via the District Inspectors. If targets are not achieved, somebody – somewhere along the chain of command – will be asking awkward questions and the shortfall will have to be satisfactorily explained.

The internal organisation of district work may vary but within each district. The District Inspector will normally have one or more Inspectors assisting who have completed a full three year training course and who have passed the Board's Commission examination and hold a certificate to that effect. The District Inspector and his fully trained colleagues will concentrate on the larger investigation cases and company and group company cases. Working to the District Inspector will be an Inspector of the Inspector (S) grade who, like the rest of the Inspectors in the district, will have only received a shorter period of training and will not have passed the Board's Commission examination. The main duties of the Inspectors (S) include the organising of the Inspectors allocated to their charge and the selecting of cases from the accounts that they screen either for in-depth reviews or perhaps in correspondence to query obvious errors in the computations submitted with the accounts. A typical district could have three or more Inspectors, plus as many more trainee Inspectors, all spending a substantial amount of their time on investigation work. The management of the clerical staff will be dealt with by separate Inspectors answerable to the District Inspector. The target figures for settlements could be 120 individual and partnership cases and some 12 company cases. These targets are for *settlements*, and, as cases can take from eighteen months to over five years to reach the settlement stage, there must always be a greater number of working cases than the target settlement figures. However, the target does mean that a minimum number of additional cases each year, equivalent to the target settlement figures, must be undertaken.

Although the length of training of the different grades of Inspectors may vary, they should all be trained and effective investigators with the full backing of the District, plus Regional and Head Office facilities and experience. The perception, resourcefulness and dogged determination of the investigators should not be underestimated if you value your money and, in extreme cases, your freedom.

Getting Selected for Investigation

The selection of cases for in-depth investigation will depend on a number of factors such as the flow of accounts received, the number that need to be selected and the number of cases that have already been pre-selected (and the file marked accordingly). If there is a surfeit of selectable cases, the most promising cases will be passed through for investigation and a prominent note made in the files of the others to look at them again next time around. There is, therefore, an element of luck in whether or not you have been or will be selected for an in-depth review. This only extends however to those cases deemed suitable for selection. If your affairs are organised so that you do not figure in that group, you should never be the subject of a Revenue accounts investigation.

Some cases are pre-selected for investigation because of information in the Revenue files. The information may emanate from:

● a statutory return – by a bank for instance;
● an anonymous 'well wisher', an upset wife, companion, relative or employee;
● another Revenue office dealing with a client, customer, or supplier where the nature of the transaction suggests some irregularity may have taken place;
● a newspaper report or article implying dubious business practice;
● anybody who may have information concerning your affairs and returns or volunteers it to the tax office;
● other investigations, either in the same or another tax office, which are pertinent to your business and suggest that some irregularity may have occurred.

It is appreciated in the tax office that the weight, accuracy, and relevance of information can vary, but once curiosity is aroused the chances are that your papers will be under regular review – even if you are not taken up immediately as an enquiry case. A completely unfounded allegation from an anonymous informant can, therefore, place you in some jeopardy.

Other cases are selected on merit. The accounts may be based on incomplete business records and include a number of estimates and perhaps a balancing figure in order to balance the cash account. There may be a clue to the nature and accuracy of the business records in the wording of the accountant's certificate given to the accounts or by reference to district experience of the type of client attracted to the particular accountant's practice. Some accountants have been investigated by the Inland Revenue Enquiry Branch and any shortcomings in their work will have been reported to the local districts to which the accountant submits accounts. Thus the standing of an accountant can have a bearing on whether or not his client may be selected for an in-depth investigation.

The more usual reason for selection is that the Revenue considers to be unsatisfactory a gross profit percentage for the particular business and locality concerned – normally coupled with what appears to be an unsatisfactory drawings figure. This means that a business is not making what it should and its owner is living on fresh air!

The Revenue produce 'Business Economic Notes' for use by Inspectors in evaluating the accuracy of the accounts of various businesses. Copies of these notes are available to taxpayers; however, there is additional confidential information – not contained in the notes available to taxpayers – that outlines possible lines of enquiry the Inspector may follow in tackling the accounts of specific businesses. Anticipate that the Inspector may be very well informed concerning *your* business.

Other clues can suggest that an investigation may be fruitful such as substantial amounts of capital being introduced, the source of which is not apparent either from your declared income, investments, or from savings made and reflected on your income tax returns. A brief description of the source of monies introduced in the letter or the computations accompanying your accounts can avoid unwelcome attention. However, it is possible that the source attributed to the funds could provoke even closer scrutiny of your affairs.

There is a chance that the local tax office may target a particular trade or activity that has given rise to substantial investigation settlements. Business accounts showing similar tendencies may well be investigated. There is also the possibility of a bank or somebody else innocently submitting incorrect information concerning your affairs, due perhaps to the careless filing of information relating to another taxpayer in your file, that could give rise to an investigation. It should not happen but it has happened – and satisfactory settlements have resulted from such initially ill-founded investigations. The inference is that if everybody in business received a telegram stating 'flee the country all is known', 99.9 per cent would go. Similarly it is felt that a random selection of accounts for in-depth examination would produce similar results to the selective system. The fact of the matter in practice is that anybody in business may find themselves on the receiving end of a Revenue investigation and you owe it to yourself and your family to be familiar with this area of the business world – just in case you are selected.

The Enquiry Branch and Special Office

If you (or your partner or co-director) have been extremely 'indiscreet', your affairs may warrant the attention of the Enquiry Branch or Special Office. These particular branches specialise in the largest and most complex cases. They are however staffed by Inspectors drawn from the districts, normally in the early stages of their careers. Their specialisation and facilities for investigation make them a formidable challenge but you should not lose sight of the fact that you could also come across the same individuals serving as District Inspectors in local districts after they have completed a term in Head Office. Your accountant, if well informed, should be aware of the officers in his or her area who have served in the Enquiry Branch or Special Office – forewarned is forearmed.

The Initial Review

Having selected a case for a possible in-depth investigation, the Inspector will review your income tax returns for a period of years. The returns will be evaluated to estimate the likely level of your private expenditure and capital accretion or diminution as the case may be. This is essentially a very hit and miss exercise, since, for example, collection of jewellery, furs, antiques and old masters will not figure on your tax returns. The current returns do not even indicate the size of your family but merely whether you are single or married. If you own a property or properties their aquisition should be shown on your income tax returns and any mortgage interest payable should also be recorded, so with local knowledge of areas and property prices the capital invested can be estimated in broad terms.

The voters list will contain details of all adult voters resident in your property at the October qualifying date. Details of planning applications can indicate some alterations or improvements to properties. A visual inspection of the property may reveal further details of the general level of affluence exhibited. The size of the garden may indicate a need to employ a gardener and the premises couid point to the presence of domestic employees. Stables, boats, car stickers and badges may also provide additional information for consideration when estimating levels of private expenditure. The nature of the vehicles in the accounts and available to the directors/proprietors will also give an indication of the life-style and image that is desired and projected. You should not assume that the Inspector is chair bound and will not either personally view your property, or arrange for another member of staff to carry out the inspection.

An external inspection of business premises can also be helpful in assessing the full range of business activities being undertaken – and whether or not they are properly reflected in the accounts that have been submitted.

The PAYE scheme can be reviewed to see if the wages charged in the accounts correspond to the amounts on which PAYE has been operated. Discrepancies would have to be looked at to see if casual, unsupported cash payments or drawings have been charged as wages. Employees' returns may be examined to see if the addresses or job descriptions indicate that private domestic employees and gardeners are being charged as business expenses. If your spouse is shown as an employee, the bona fides of the employment and the precise nature of her duties – and their worth to the business – may have to be considered. The same consideration applies to sons' and daughters' wages charged to the business.

The drawings from the business will be considered. In many cases the information regarding drawings is incomplete and a summary of the drawings account may not have been submitted with the business accounts. The Inspector will aim to reconstruct the drawings position year by year over a period of years to see what pattern emerges. If, for example, you are taking out lower amounts than your salaried employees, the Inspector may wonder why you are paying employees more than you pay yourself.

The business accounts may be summarised for a period of years, the comparative figures being examined to detect inconsistencies in such entries as levels of debtors, creditors, stock, turnover, wages, gross profit percentages made on sales. The Inspector will list the items that have attracted attention and in his or her view, call for an explanation. When the review has been completed the Inspector will decide whether or not to challenge the accuracy of your income tax returns and accounts. The challenge will normally be by letter, stating that the Inspector is not satisfied with your accounts and/or income tax returns and specifying, in broad terms, why he or she is not satisfied and what additional information and/or documents are required. This request will usually be coupled with a further request that you call with your accountant to see the Inspector at the tax office.

The point to make at this stage is that the information available to the Inspector at the time the interview is requested is normally pretty sketchy. If you have been foolish enough to omit some obvious item of income from your income tax returns then the Inspector can point to that as proof positive that you have been negligent in completing your returns and that there are valid grounds for checking that there is nothing else amiss. If you have been rash enough to sign blank returns for completion by your accountant and your accuntant's clerk has failed to record an item of income, or if there has been some other failure in communication leading to an omission, the neglect involved cannot be passed on to your accountant. You are personally responsible for the accuracy of your returns and cannot transfer that responsibility to anybody else. The only area for which there can be any possible excuse relates to income of your wife. If you have asked your wife about her income from each of the sources listed on your income tax return and have correctly recorded the information you received, you cannot be asked to do any more. If, however, your wife is a partner or director in your business or company then the omission of wife's income could be claimed to indicate the possibility of irregularities in the business accounts.

With the advent of independent taxation for married women from 5 April 1990, all wives are now responsible for making any necessary income tax returns, and for giving notification of chargeability to tax from 1990/91 onwards. The Courts have defined a 'wife' for income tax purposes as someone who has entered into a lawful marriage with a particular man. [See: Rignell (Inspector of Taxes) V Andrews No. 3229.]

The Steps of the Ritual Dance
If the Inspector puts the reasons for his dissatisfaction with the accounts in general terms, you should ask for them to be particularised in precise detail so that your accountant, with your assistance, can answer them. This is the start of the ritual dance through which each in- vestigation progresses, the steps of which being normally unknown to taxpayers puts them at a grave disadvantage.

The statutory background is, like all taxation topics, complex. Basically, assessments are made on business profits at various dates by the Inspector of Taxes at times convenient to his or her staff. However, the aim is that the assessments will all be issued, and the thirty day appeal time limit will have expired, prior to the due date of payment of the tax specified on the notice of assessment. Your accountant may have submitted your accounts prior to the assessment being made, in which case in the situation outlined the Inspector will express dissatisfaction with the accounts as provided for in Section 29 of the Taxes Management Act 1970 (TMA1970) and 'make an assessment to tax to the best of his judgement'. That means that he will raise an assessment in excess of the amount justified by your accounts. Your only redress is to appeal against the assessment and to ask for the postponement of the amount of the tax which you consider to be excessive. Alternatively, if no accounts are available to the Inspector at the time when the assessment is made, he will make an assessment in an amount 'which ought in his opinion to be charged'. Again, redress is only by way of an appeal against the assessment so you are effectively in the same situation. It does not take a lawyer to appreciate that 'to the best of his judgement' and 'ought in his opinion to be charged' both give the Inspector sufficient power to make an assessment which is bound to provoke an appeal.

Once an appeal is received Pandora's box has been opened and can only be closed either by the settlement of the appeal by the agreement of the figures between the Inspector and the taxpayer, or by the determination of the assessment by the General or Special Commissioners – with the possibility of the appeal going on a point of law through the High Court, the Court of Appeal, and finally the House of Lords. Very few appeals are, in fact, litigated through the courts both because of the expense and of the uncertainty of the outcome. The costs of the hearings, from the Commissioners onwards, follow the final decision – so if you lose, it can be very expensive.

Obtaining Information and Documents

Once an appeal has been lodged the initiative passes to the Inspector who can, in the absence of satisfactory progress, list the appeal for hearing by the General Commissioners. The idea is not normally to determine the appeal but to enable the Inspector to ask the Commissioners to issue a precept under the provisions of Section 51 TMA1970. This section is very important and reads:

(1) The Commissioners may at any time before the determination of an appeal give notice to the appellant or other party to the proceedings (not being an inspector or the Board) requiring him within the time specified in the notice–
   (a) to deliver to them such particulars as they may require for the purpose of determining the appeal, and
   (b) to make available for inspection by them, or by any officer of the Board, all such books, accounts or other documents in his possession or power as may be specified or described in the notice, being books, accounts or other documents which, in the opinion of the Commissioners issuing the notice, contain or may contain information relating to the subject matter of the proceedings.
(2) Any officer of the Board may, at all reasonable times, inspect and take copies of, or extracts from, any particulars delivered under subsection(1)(a) above; and the Commissioners or any officer of the Board may take copies of, or extracts from, any books, accounts, or other documents made available for their or his inspection under subsection(1)1(b) above.

In practice, under the particulars heading the Inspector can (through the Commissioners) require you to produce capital, income, and expenditure statements, and indeed any 'such particulars as they may require for the purpose of determining the appeal'. 'They' are the Commissioners, but in practice the Inspector initiates the procedure. The Commissioners normally know nothing about the case until the appeal is brought before them, and the appellant and/or an adviser appear before them. It is not unknown for Commissioners to exceed their powers and to issue illegal precepts. There is no easy remedy for this in law and, if your adviser can make no impact on the Commissioners or their Clerk, it is likely to be more cost-effective to comply with the precept.

The Commissioners are aware of the investigation procedures adopted by the Inspector, and, in my experience, it is sufficient to explain to the Commissioners, at the hearing, that the accounts are under investigation to obtain the Commissioners' signatures to a pre-drafted precept, or precepts. The production of '. . . all such books, accounts or other documents . . . relating to the subject matter of the proceedings' should bring forth any items requested by the Inspector in correspondence that have not been produced. Indeed, a little thought will quickly bring home to you the awesome extent of the Commissioners' powers to require any particulars and documents, and, for all practical purposes, those powers devolve to the Inspector.

The Inspector has further extensive powers in his armoury under Section 20 TMA1970. The Inspector, with the consent of a Commissioner, may require you to deliver any documents you can which he or she feels are relevant to the investigation. In addition, he has the power to insist that an accountant found guilty of any tax offence in a UK court or penalised under the provisions of Section 99 TMA1970, produce any documents relevant to the tax liability of any client. I have not detailed the full powers available to the Inspector because this book is aiming to sketch out, in practical and understandable terms, the range of legislation available to the Inspector. There is no future in trying to fight the Revenue system – accept that the Inspector enjoys sweeping powers to obtain particulars and documents. Co-operate on your terms and do not try to fight the system – it is too expensive and, in my view, counter-productive.

Your Personal Involvement in the Enquiry
It is essential that you become personally involved in the Inspector's enquiries at an early stage, preferably asking the Inspector to forward copies of all letters issued to your accountant to you. If you follow this practice you will become aware of any unnecessary delays on the part of your accountant and can take appropriate action. The last thing you want is for your accountant to neglect your affairs, causing you to be dubbed uncooperative by the Inspector. It is often only when an

investigation opens and positive constructive action is called for that you find that you have been employing an inefficient and/or incompetent accountant. If your accountant is too busy preparing accounts for other clients to give your affairs the attention they deserve, I can only suggest that you change your accountant – sooner rather than later.

It is not exceptional for taxpayers to find that precepts have been issued by General Commissioners because of delays directly attributable to their accountants. Such accountants are not usually responsive to any representations from any quarter and should be dropped without delay. If you have been foolish enough to persevere with such an accountant and find matters getting out of hand, you can try attending the Commissioners' meetings to explain your difficulties to them in person. The Commissioners do have the power to issue witness summons to accountants to attend, but tend to consider that it is up to taxpayers to ensure that they are properly represented.

Never lose sight of the fact that it is *your* affairs that are being looked into by the Revenue. You will be personally responsible for any neglect or errors that have occurred and the bill at the end of the day for any tax lost, interest and penalties – plus accountancy fees – will be yours. Make sure you get an efficient, cost-effective service and, remember, a long enquiry is an expensive enquiry.

If you fail to give the Revenue enquiries the attention that they warrant, you could find yourself bearing penalties awarded for failing to comply with precepts. Such payments will give you no benefit. They will not reduce any eventual settlement figure; indeed, they provide evidence of non-cooperation and lead to larger penalties being imposed in respect of any tax lost.

The accountant is your professional adviser. There is no point in paying for advice if you do not take it. If you are not totally *au fait* with what is going on and how your accountant envisages the enquiry progressing, you should ask your accountant for a full explanation of the situation. Your accountant should be aware of any weaknesses in the business records and should be able to carry out his own investigation to pre-empt what the Inspector may discover and give you advice on how best to present the facts to the Inspector. However, the accountant will charge for this service and it can be quite expensive. The easier you make this task, the lower the fees will be. If you are aware of what is likely to emerge from the Revenue enquiry then you must decide to what extent you wish to confide in your accountant. You should consider just how heinous your offence may be considered and what evidence of it is likely to exist. Once you make a disclosure to your accountant, he or she should be guided by a professional code of conduct and may, therefore, be inhibited in acting on your behalf in the way that you desire.

You cannot expect accountants to put their professional reputations and careers in jeopardy to assist you in deceiving the Revenue.

You may go to a solicitor for advice if you are aware that serious irregularities are about to be unearthed. This could give to you the opportunity of discussing your position frankly, without involving your accountant or committing yourself to a particular, and irrevocable, course of action.

2   The Opening Interview

If you attend the tax office with your accountant at the Inspector's request you will find yourself involved in a very detailed review of your business, its records, and your involvement in its conduct. Your private capital income and expenditure position will also be explored. The opening procedure at the interview will give you some idea of the course that it is likely to follow. If your attention is drawn to the form 94M it means that the Inspector feels that there is sufficient information to justify asking you to make a full and frank disclosure of all irregularities in which he or she considers you have been implicated. However, if you are given a copy of the Hansard extract setting out the terms of the Chancellor of the Exchequer's statement concerning alleged frauds on the Revenue, then the Inspector may be considering the possibility of your eventual prosecution. The purpose of the Hansard leaflet is to make admissible in evidence any statement that you may make, regardless of the implied inducements contained in the Chancellor's statement. If the Inspector asks you prepared questions and records your replies verbatim after giving the usual warning in accordance with the 'judge's rules', then you are in deep trouble.

The Hansard Extract
The Hansard statement of 5 October 1944 is:

> The practice of the Commissioners in this matter is governed by s.34 of the FA1942, which makes provision for the admissibility in evidence of any disclosure made in the circumstances there set out. As the section indicates, the Commissioners have a general power under which they can accept pecuniary settlements instead of instituting criminal proceedings in respect of fraud or wilful default alleged to have been committed by a taxpayer. They can, however, give no undertaking to a taxpayer in any such case that they will accept such a settlement and refrain from instituting criminal proceedings even if the case is one in which the taxpayer has made full confession and has given full facilities for investigation of the facts. They reserve to themselves complete discretion in all cases as to the

course which they will pursue, but it is their practice to be influenced by the fact that the taxpayer has made a full confession and has given full facilities for investigation into his affairs and for examination of such books, papers, documents or information as the Commissioners may consider necessary.

After reading the Hansard extract you will be read Section 105 of the TMA1970:

(1) Statements made or documents produced by or on behalf of a person shall not be inadmissible in any such proceedings as are mentioned in subsection (2) below by reason only that it has been drawn to his attention that-
    (a) pecuniary settlements may be accepted instead of a penalty being determined, or proceedings being instituted, in relation to any tax, and
    (b) though no undertaking can be given as to whether or not the Board will accept such a settlement in the case of any particular person, it is the practice of the Board to be influenced by the fact that a person has made a full confession of any fraudulent conduct to which he had been a party and has given full facilities for investigation, and that he was or may have been induced thereby to make the statements or produce the documents.
(2) The proceedings mentioned in subsection (1) above are-
    (a) any criminal proceedings against the person in question for any form of fraudulent conduct in connection with or in relation to tax, and
    (b) any proceedings against him for the recovery of any tax due from him, whether by way of tax or penalty, in connection with or in relation to tax, and
    (c) any proceedings for a penalty or an appeal against the determination of a penalty.

After the Hansard extract has been read to you, you will be asked to confirm that you understand what has been said. If you claim not to understand, it will simply be re-read until you do understand the statement. The Inspector is not permitted to paraphrase or to explain the statement in case he or she unwittingly makes the evidence that you give inadmissible by suggesting that a full and frank confession will advance your cause – thereby offering an inducement for your evidence. You must appreciate that it is a criminal offence to submit false accounts to defraud the Inland Revenue and/or to conspire with others to that end. A non-statutory form 94M, sometimes used to advise taxpayers of the practice of the Board in accepting monetary settlements, should not be used for the more serious cases, as it is considered to offer an inducement to confess, and would make any confession obtained inadmissible in evidence.

The Hansard extract and the formal warning that you are not obliged to say anything, but what you do say will be taken down in writing and given in evidence, are normally only used by Enquiry Branch or Special Office staff who specialise in serious fraud cases. However, there are occasions when the District Inspector may wish to use the formal procedure appropriate to the more serious cases.

You may be given certain questions in writing after you have been read the Hansard extract. The questions basically ask you to confirm in writing that you are satisfied that all your income tax returns and business accounts are correct and complete. You will also be asked to confirm that you are prepared to give full access to all your business and private records so that the Revenue may be satisfied that your answers to the other questions are correct. The procedure of putting these questions in writing to taxpayers has received the approval of the Courts. You will not usually be asked for immediate replies to the questions, but will be asked to go away and carefully consider the questions before committing yourself in writing. This procedure can be disconcerting and is calculated to produce a disclosure from the taxpayer of the irregularities in which he is considered to have been involved. You may be asked to let the Inspector have your replies to the questions within ten days or so. In any event, a timetable for the submission of your replies and a follow-up meeting will be specified.

The Inspector's Review of Business Records
Prior to the interview, or possibly during the course of it, the Inspector is likely to examine your business records. He or she is also likely to have already put questions in writing to your accountant regarding the nature and amount of any balancing figures or estimates that had to be employed in drawing up the accounts and whether or not there are any reserves or provisions not shown on the face of the balance sheets. A copy of the cash and bank reconciliation may also be requested. These questions are designed to highlight any weakness in your business records.

The Inspector will not normally seek to re-audit or veritfy the accuracy of the work carried out by your accountant. There is not a lot of time to be spent on the examination of records so the time spent must be cost-effective – carrying out spot checks that your accountant will not have employed. Your accountant may accept without question the allocation of expenditure that you have adopted in entering items of expenditure in your Cash Book or Petty Cash Book, confining his attention to the invoices that refer to the Cash Book and Petty Cash Book entries. The Inspector will devote more attention to the description of the purchases shown on the invoices, seeking to identify private items of expenditure that have not been charged to drawings. He will also be interested in the wages charge, particularly in any casual wages passing through the Petty Cash Book with little or no independent supporting evidence that the money has actually been paid out to bona fide employees.

Attention may be directed to vehicle repair bills and fuel invoices. It may emerge that the vehicle featuring on some of the invoices is not a business vehicle. The mileage details shown on repair bills may indicate that the bulk of the mileage clocked up occurs in the holiday months, and AA foreign travel insurance cover may feature on the invoices. Such details could show that adjustments to eliminate private mileage expenditure from the total car expenses are inadequate.

Property repair bills may show that the work has been carried out on private, not business, premises. Private expenditure on such items as various electrical goods, wine and spirits, and so on have all figured in business purchases over the years and have not been charged to drawings.

Drawings are not always properly or fully recorded. On occasion the drawings figure is just a balancing figure. In other cases the allocation of drawings throughout the year may show that you have apparently only drawn specific cheques and have no cash available to meet your private expenditure. Alternatively, you may be living like a lord for three months and starving for the rest of the year. So, though the aggregate figure may look alright, its make-up may not stand up to close scrutiny.

The sales figures may show repetitive, round sum estimates or have some days, weeks, or months when there are no sales at all. There may be unusually large purchases at the year end that are not apparently reflected in the stock figures. On an annual basis, sales less cash expenditure from sales may balance with the bankings but produce a negative cash in hand figure when a cash flow computation is made for part of the year.

The Inspector will have a critical comprehensive look at your business records. The aim is to show that there is something wrong or not quite right with your books, records, accounts, and income tax returns. Once that has been established, the onus passes to you to demonstrate that you have made a full and correct return of all your income or, alternatively, to identify and quantify the nature and amount of any errors or omissions.

The Inspector may examine printers' dates of publication of stationery as part of his review of your records. It is not unknown, for instance, for allegedly contemporary Cash Books and so on to carry a printer's date of a year more recent than the year claimed to be involved. Such discrepancies can undermine the evidential value of the records concerned. You must, therefore, expect all your records to be examined in what may seem to be a rather novel and unexpected way.

The Position of the Accountant

Before we continue with the interview at the Inspector's office, let us consider the position of the accountant *vis-à-vis* the client. The accountant is a member of a profession, with professional standards and a code of conduct to uphold. Accountants vary considerably in their own standards of behaviour but, once an investigation has commenced into your affairs and it is established that you have been guilty of an offence, you are on your own. It would be a very exceptional and foolish accountant who would be prepared to conspire with a client to defraud the Revenue although this has, of course, happened on rare occasions. After all, unless the accountant is personally benefiting from the frauds and not just receiving fees for preparing accounts, he has nothing to gain from being a party to any guilty knowledge. On the contrary he has everything to lose – even more than the taxpayer perpetrating the frauds – because as a professional person he is likely to be more harshly treated by the Courts and also to be disciplined by his own professional body. He may indeed be obliged to cease in practice altogether as an accountant.

If, when your accountant first contacts you about the Inspector's challenge to your accounts, you wish to make a full disclosure to your accountant and obtain his professional help, you should appreciate that the only advice he can give is for you to make a full and frank disclosure to the Revenue. If you do not choose to make such a disclosure then your accountant should cease to act on your behalf. Needless to say, an accountant resigning from a case when accounts are challenged or a taxpayer going to a new accountant at the beginning or during the course of an enquiry can indicate to the Inspector that there are bigger and better disclosures to follow – or to be dug out.

Your accountant, who may have tacitly gone along with dubious business records etc., will not wish to be tainted by any suggestion of malpractice. He or she will wish to assume the pose of injured innocence and, indeed, some accountants have been genuinely hurt and offended at being misled by clients. You are, therefore, as I have already said, quite on your own and devoid of the assistance and guidance that you would wish for at this stage in your affairs. What you need is an independent personal adviser, who has not been involved in the production of your accounts, to indicate what is likely to emerge in the course of an investigation of your affairs and the minimum amount that can be established as having been misappropriated.

The Interview Notes
Returning to the interview at the Inspector's office he will in all probability advise you that he will be making notes of the information that you give during the course of the interview and arrange to send to you two copies of his notes so that you can sign, date and return one copy of the notes to confirm that they correctly set out the information given. If any amendments are considered appropriate, these can be made prior to signature. If, on reflection, you feel that you wish to volunteer additional information or to amend or amplify any statement made, such additional comments should be contained in a supplementary note to the agreed interview notes. The procedure of agreeing interview notes is the best way the Inspector can ensure that any errors or mis-understandings at the interview are corrected and that a permanent record of the information you have supplied is made.

Your veracity as a possible witness is central to your defence. If it can be demonstrated that you have given incorrect information, or told a deliberate lie, then the chance of your insubstantiated word being believed concerning any other aspect of your affairs is very slim indeed. The agreed interview notes are designed to tie you down to a particular account of events before you become fully aware what amounts and years the Revenue is interested in. If you make unguarded and ill-considered statements at this point, the Revenue can later use them to destroy your credibility as a witness.

The Inspector will wish to build up as complete a picture of your personal and business affairs as possible to enable him to satisfy himself that your taxation affairs are in order. The initial cause of dissatisfaction with your accounts and/or taxation returns can be used as an excuse for a very wide-ranging 'fishing expedition'. A refusal to discuss your personal affairs may be taken by the Inspector as a lack of co-operation – which can leave you not knowing where you can *safely* draw the veil on the grounds that the requested information is nothing to do either with the Inspector or your business affairs.

Basically, the Revenue will wish to ensure that you have been able to finance the purchase or acquisition of all your assets and to have met your personal expenditure either from known and correctly declared sources of taxable income, or from bona fide non-taxable sources. If there are, for example, amounts necessary to fund:

● the purchase of assets;
● bank deposits;

18

- building society or other savings accounts;
- the cost of private expenditure;

for which you cannot account, the Revenue will assume that your money came from undeclared taxable income. It will be left to you to show that the monies came from non-taxable sources.

The Revenue's starting point is, therefore, a review of your assets and liabilities, and you should be aware of the items that can spring to mind. Most people have bank, building society and savings accounts of various descriptions so let us assume that you will be asked for details of all such accounts. It may be that the Inspector has become aware of the existence of some of the accounts prior to the interview. He may wish for a very detailed reply by including in his request details of *all* accounts whether in your own name, in joint names, or in any name or names of convenience. If you have opened an account in a family name other than your own or in a purely ficticious name, such a question puts you in the immediate dilemma of having to make your mind up on the spur of the moment either to disclose or to conceal the account. Just suppose, for the sake of argument, that you have been engaged in some activity that you wish to conceal (for personal reasons) from relatives and associates and have opened an account in a fictitious name solely for that purpose. It may be that you do not wish to disclose the account to your accountant or to the Inspector, feeling that it is none of their business. Faced with a direct question bearing on the matter, you have three options. You can:

- disclose the account;
- omit to mention the account;
- refuse to answer the question.

If you disclose the account, supplementary questions are likely to follow, and the full reason for and the use made of the account or accounts will be explored in depth. The Inspector may assume that the account has been opened to facilitate the extraction of business monies and the understatement of taxable profits. Any claim to non-taxable receipts you make will have to be substantiated by evidence acceptable to the Inspector. Claims of betting wins, monetary gifts from deceased friends and relatives, or to having sold various heirlooms and so on are likely to be greeted with some scepticism – if not derision – and rejected out of hand. Accounts that involve gifts from others may invite a request for details of the names and addresses, with resulting follow-up enquiries addressed to the donors. The possibility of such action, and its embarrassing consequences, may be sufficient to provoke a spurious and incorrect explanation for the source of the monies. You are then engaged in the process of destroying your own credibility – your only defence in the absence of finite evidence.

If you omit to disclose an account, you are taking a conscious decision to mislead the Inspector, for whatever reason, and discovery can lead to undesirable results. A close scrutiny of other accounts and transactions may reveal the existence of the undisclosed account, by virtue of transactions passing through disclosed accounts. In addition, if the undisclosed account has been used to finance the purchase of an asset or assets or to meet recurring expenses, those transactions may point to the existence of an undisclosed account – or to an additional source of undisclosed income. These matters need considerable forethought and research prior to the interview.

A refusal to answer the Inspector's questions would be taken as a refusal to co-operate with the Revenue in their enquiries. The Inspector would assume the worst and proceed using his statutory powers, possibly involving the making of estimated assessments that you may consider grossly excessive, listing any appeals for hearing by the Commissioners, and seeking precepts under the provisions of Section 51 of the TMA1970. Once a precept has been issued you must either comply with it to the best of your ability or face ongoing penalties for failing to comply, until the Commissioners are satisfied that you have supplied all the particulars and/or documents specified as are within your knowledge, possession or control. Resistance is quite pointless: it involves nothing but unproductive expense on your part. The Revenue enquiry will proceed with or without your willing co-operation. Therefore, you really only have two alternatives – correct answers or deliberate concealment.

Other obvious questions concern deposit boxes of all types. The Inspector knows that business people have made a habit of extracting funds from their businesses, either by understating sales of one form or another, or overstating purchases or wages and so on. The ill-gotten gains, if not immediately spent, have to be retained in a safe place. The obvious place is a bank or building society but, since this method involves a record of the deposit, the anonymous deposit box is a possible alternative – and the Inspector is likely to ask about your use of such facilities. Also it should be noted that the bank may have debited your personal account for the use of the deposit box facility. It is also possible that at some stage you may be asked to give to the Inspector an authority to approach your bank manager. Such an authority is likely to be couched in wide terms that will ask your bank manager to supply details of all your accounts and business conducted on your behalf, including facilities provided such as deposit boxes, travellers cheques, foreign currency purchases, and dealings in securities. The manager may also be asked about other accounts that he had become aware of through the internal workings of the bank. It is an obvious advantage if there are no nasty skeletons rattling about in the cupboard!

The desire to keep 'tax free' cash away from bank accounts and similar places of safety can lead to large amounts of cash being kept about the house. Everybody is aware of the various home safes that are available, especially local villains. Newspaper reports of amounts alleged to have been lost in burglaries, in cash and other valuables, and/or leaks to the Revenue can spark off enquiries into the victims' taxation affairs. Safe deposit boxes have not been immune from the attentions of the criminal fraternity but they have at least appeared to give some anonymity to those hiring the boxes.

Unbanked cash is an item that the Inspector is likely to ask about specifically. You may be asked, for instance, how much you actually have with you at the interview and what other amounts are held elsewhere. To get a representative picture you may be asked about the amounts normally drawn in cash and how they are utilised: giving details of the approximate maximum amount ever held, describing the circumstances giving rise to that exceptional amount and the approximate date held. The idea is to restrict the parameters available to you and your advisers to transpose cash from surplus years to deficiency years at a later date.

The list of assets that the Inspector may explore is virtually endless. Property in the UK or elsewhere is a distinct possibility. Such assets may give rise to rental income of course, and it is normal to have overseas bank accounts to manage overseas property. Holiday properties and caravans give rise to similar possibilities. Letting may also be home centred and is quite common in holiday, language school, and university town areas. It has become particularly fashionable to offer for rent surplus farm and cottage accommodation. The Revenue questions are likely to be tailored to the particular circumstances of the case under investigation.

The Inspector will also be aware of the amounts being expended in auction rooms in the desire to maintain if not increase the value of cash not immediately required to meet personal needs. Some trades or activities lend themselves to hobby activities such as vehicle restoration or the collection of antiques and precious metal coins. Such activities are likely to be covered by the Inspector in any review of personal assets. The more common involvement in stocks and shares is likely to be dealt with at the interview. Again note that traces of share transactions are likely to be reflected in bank statements. Speculative questions about boats, and home extensions and improvements may also be asked.

Private incomings and expenditure details are normally sought and the questions asked may cover such items as gifts made or received. A positive response will prompt further questions: details of the dates, amounts, and background to such transactions, and the bank or other accounts in which they appear. Private expenditure details may be requested including such items as the full make up of the household – the number of children and other dependants; a broad outline of the division of the household bills between husbands and wives or partners; and details of any housekeeping allowance. In addition the ages of the children may be recorded, together with supplementary information concerning school fees. Expenditure on holidays will be queried, you may be asked to produce your passport with a view to seeing what, if any, visa stamps are shown and the dates of the holidays involved. The Inspector may ask for details of the insurance premiums you pay. A request to see the household policy may follow as the policy could include a schedule itemising valuable assets such as jewellery, antiques and furs.

The Interview Follow Up
At the conclusion of the interview you may be asked if there is any other information that you wish to volunteer, just in case the Inspector may have forgotten something or you want to subsequently claim that you would have been happy to disclose an additional source of income if you had only been asked! He is then likely to outline the additional information and documents that he may want to complete his enquiries. This is likely to be the beginning of a long and expensive correspondence, with documents and information supplied leading to yet more requests for still more information and documents.

You may find that the enquiry into the current year's accounts is extended to earlier years. The Inspector will seek to identify the sources of all the various credits to your bank and investment accounts and the purposes for which cheques were drawn, identifying the expenditure involved. Summaries of your bank and investment accounts may be requested together with bank statements, cheque stubs and paying-in books. It is always a good idea to keep copies of your bank statements covering a six year period to avoid the expense and inconvenience of having to obtain duplicate statements from the bank.

Depending on the outcome of the Inspector's initial enquiries and examination of your records, the Inspector may ask you to authorise your accountant to prepare capital, income, and expenditure statements in respect of your personal affairs, if he considers that irregularities have been established. If he has not found any specific irregularities but is still not satisfied with your accounts, the Inspector may seek the necessary information to enable him to draw up capital, income, and expenditure statements himself. The statements can involve not only summarising all bank and investment accounts but also constructing a separate balanced cash account. This procedure is exactly the same as that used in preparing your business accounts. The outcome is an annual balance sheet showing your personal assets, including unbanked cash and liabilities, and identifying the make up of your net wealth. The appropriate corresponding profit and loss account will also be prepared in respect of your personal affairs showing your incomings from all sources, whether taxable or not, and your private outgoings. Like your business accounts, the net increase or decrease in your capital worth for any particular year or period should reconcile with the net available from your incomings less outgoings. Needless to say, there may be a discrepancy or two.

The discrepancies may arise from incomings, identified in bank or building society accounts and so on, that cannot be shown to have come from declared and/or known sources. The same situation may apply to amounts spent on acquiring assets, that have come from unidentified sources. On the expenditure side discrepancies can arise from known recurring expenditure that has not been financed from indentified sources. In so far as these are cash items they will all be swept into the cash account.

3   Alternatives to the Opening Interview

We have considered the mechanics, now let us consider the flesh and blood.

Each investigation saga has its roots in the information, accounts, and returns submitted to the tax office. In the tax office, targets will have been set and the Inspectors will be looking for the softest, most lucrative, cases available. Since individual Inspectors are judged by the results that they produce and not by any elegantly conducted near misses, the pressure to succeed is strong. Nothing speaks louder than results and the Inspector who fails to produce the goods will not advance. The same measure is passed on up through the chain of command, so a District failing to meet its investigation target is seen as a black mark for the District Inspector. The District result is reflected in the Group's figures, and so casts a shadow on the Group Controller. If it is bad enough to effect the Region's results, the failure also rebounds upon the Regional Controller. The outcome is that everybody is keen to produce results and to meet targets – which is fine provided that you are not a target!

The Inspector investigating your tax affairs will be looking for an early breakthrough in his enquiry. The best way to tackle any investigation is to examine all the papers and information available to you, summarising the details year by year. It may be assumed that some information has been received to bring your file to the top of the pile. Alternatively you may have become complacent about your drawings position, to such an extent that the Inspector feels that there must be some error or understatement in your accounts, that can be brought to light with the minimum of effort. He will also wish to ensure that you are sufficiently cash, or asset rich to fund a settlement. After all, he is thinking in terms of a monetary payment for his statistics, and if you have no money there will be complications for the Revenue in agreeing an acceptable means of settlement. A shortage of funds also stiffens the resolve of the taxpayer to refute the Inspector's claims. The taxpayer is, no doubt, already disappointed by his lack of business success and to have the Inspector poised to take away what little he has and perhaps thrust him into debt, is not an appealing prospect. The taxpayer probably thinks the Inspector would be better employed spending his time investigating someone else but that will hardly alleviate his immediate problem. Some taxpayers, however, so bubble with resentment that they do supply information concerning other taxpayers. Needless so say, such action does not affect the course of the enquiry into their own affairs.

So let us assume that the Inspectors have selected a taxpayer with a reasonably sized business and no foreseeable liquidity problems. The next thing to consider is the nature, and quality, of the professional assistance given to the taxpayer. Inspectors are reluctant to get involved with accountants who have a bad track record of co-operation with the Revenue. Prickly accountants who are likely to lodge a complaint with the District Inspector or the Group Controller are not to be taken on lightly. Inspectors are all human, and the District Inspector or Group Controller may – with the benefit of hindsight – suggest an alternative approach, that would have avoided the complaint. In addition, the District Inspector or Group Controller will not welcome having to become embroiled in a case for which they can claim no credit. Therefore, a complaint has no positive side as far as individual Revenue staff are concerned. Some of the irritation caused is bound to rub off on the unfortunate investigator. So far as the taxpayer is concerned, the trouble with such accountants is that they can be so bloody-minded that they are impossible for anybody to deal with, and earn a bad reputation among the Commissioners. They can also be responsible for involving the taxpayer in unnecessary accountancy fees.

Other accountants may have a reputation for poor and shoddy work, and their accounts may be considered an easy touch by the Inspector. The accountant may also be more compliant, being aware of his own shortcomings and knowing that the Inspector is familiar with his work. The accountant may have built up a good reputation with clients through his easy going manner, and unquestioning acceptance of the most improbable records and explanations. In this context, a 'good' accountant is sometimes seen as one who is ostensibly saving substantial amounts off your tax bill by his uncritical attitude. It is, however, quite straightforward to submit dubious accounts showing sub-standard profits when all the responsibility for the accuracy of the accounts rests with the taxpayer. Also, the client will accept accountancy charges more readily when the tax bill is being ameliorated.

Again let us assume that the taxpayer has a generally efficient accountant engaged in a busy practice with larger and more demanding clients than our taxpayer. The initial letter from the Inspector may, or may not, come as a surprise to the accountant. He may have wondered why his client had not been taken up for investigation years ago. Naturally he will wish to discuss the matter with his client in order to respond to the Inspector's enquiries but he will not normally wish to incur his client's displeasure by trying to undertake a full review of his client's affairs. After all, it could be difficult to justify the charges involved to his client. To be fair, unless his client is prepared to unburden himself and account for the Inspector's interest, the accountant may wait to see what emerges from a visit with his client to the tax office. Clearly the taxpayer should be in a position to answer any points raised by the Inspector without any advance priming. The difficulty is that nobody knows precisely what the Inspector will ask, or what information he may have received.

Who Pays?

It is at this stage that things can start to go wrong from the taxpayer's point of view. He is the only financial loser – the nut in the nutcracker. He will have to pay any accountancy fees incurred due to the enquiry, so the accountant is merely doing the job for which he is being paid. His only concern may be to minimise his fees and retain his client's business by keeping him relatively happy. Similarly, the Inspector will be receiving his salary and also looking to the results of the enquiry to enhance his personal standing within the Department. The taxpayer must try to continue to run his business with the additional expense and worry of the enquiry. In addition, he must deal with the Inspector's questions, some of which may seem ill-conceived and of little relevance. In a bemused and worried frame of mind, the taxpayer is persuaded that he should co-operate with the Inspector and call at the tax office with his accountant. If wise he will ask in advance what his accountant will be charging for his attendance at the interview working on an average one and a half hour interview, plus travelling time, plus follow-up consultation. The taxpayer must also take into account the loss to the business of his own time and the disruption of his day. It can be a very costly exercise. What is in it for the taxpayer? Realistically, can he hope to satisfy the Inspector at the interview that there is nothing wrong with his returns and accounts, and that his selection for investigation is a mistake? I suppose it *may* happen.

The Inspector will be looking forward to interviewing the taxpayer. He will have very little knowledge of the taxpayer's personal affairs or the business and its records. He can only know what he has been told in correspondence, or what additional details have been supplied from other, perhaps doubtful sources. He needs the taxpayer, more than the taxpayer needs the Inspector. An experienced Inspector will seek to establish all the basic facts concerning the taxpayer's private and business affairs, areas explored in Chapter 2. A technique effectively used by Inspectors is to go through all the apparently non-contentious points first, closing up possible bolt holes that might tempt the taxpayer to fabricate stories to explain any income deficiencies. If direct questions likely to antagonise the taxpayer need to be asked, the Inspector will keep them for the end of the interview, when a withdrawal of co-operation by the taxpayer will have minimal effect on the outcome of the interview.

Gathering Information

The aim of the opening interview is not to demolish the taxpayer's accounts, but rather to gather information that will enable the Inspector to thoroughly explore and record details of the taxpayer's business and private affairs, and assets. The information will then be included in interview notes with the object of obtaining written confirmation from the taxpayer after the interview that the notes correctly set out the information given. These signed notes are the sound foundation upon which the Inspector aims to build his case. If the taxpayer declines to sign the notes, the Inspector will merely write to confirm that he will rely on the accuracy of the notes in the absence of any representation from the taxpayer to correct them.

Prior to the interview the Inspector will ask fairly standard questions designed to highlight in advance any weaknesses in the business records and to establish the precise make up of those records. Of particular interest are the primary records and any informal records from which the business records are written up. He may also ask to see the business records prior to the interview, and will naturally tend to slant his questions in the direction of the weaknesses in your accounts and returns that are the basic causes for his concern. If the Inspector is lucky, the records will not stand up to close scrutiny and the private accounts will include unexplained assets not reflected in the business records.

The standard questions concern the use of estimates and balancing figures in drawing up the accounts. Most small to medium size accounts, including close private company accounts, only carry qualified certificates from the accountants. In the case of unincorporated businesses, the accountant is unlikely to have carried out a full audit. The accounts will be based on the books and records of the business, and the information and explanations supplied by the proprietor. In company cases there may be reference to the small size of the business and on the accountant's reliance on the information supplied by the directors. Therefore, the records, though considered adequate for the size of the business concerned, may not be complete or enable the accountant to independently verify certain figures. He may not have attended any stocktaking to ensure that the work was properly carried out, and that the appropriate adjustments have been made for items in transit or work in progress. That does not mean that the accountant has not carried out his duties correctly, or that the same certificate and conditions apply to all other businesses of that type and size.

The Inspector, by asking if it was possible to complete a cash reconciliation without adjustment, and if any adjustment was necessary, the amount of that adjustment and how it was dealt with in drawing up the accounts, is seeking to use the work carried out by the accountant to save himself time and effort. If the books have been properly kept and an actual count made of cash each day to reconcile the opening balance, plus cash sales, less cash outgoings, drawings and bankings, with the ending cash figure, there should be no major discrepancies on the cash account. If the records are constructed to some degree, however, and the correct figures have not been entered, the cash account may show a substantial discrepancy. When the accountant carries out his review of the cash account he could find a cash shortfall arising from a simple comparison of the relevant figures. If there is a shortfall in recorded cash sales he could finish up with a negative figure for cash in hand. No doubt he will have asked his client about the discrepancy at the time he prepared the accounts, and will have relied on his client's explanation of unrecorded sales accounting for the discrepancy. If on the other hand the computed ending cash in hand balance is much greater than that shown in the books, the accountant may have been told of unrecorded additional expenditure on business purchases. The accountant knows that the Inspector will not accept a claim for unsupported additional business purchases. If the expenditure is not backed by invoices or receipts, the Inspector will attribute the notional surplus of cash shown by the business records to unrecorded private drawings by the proprietor. The Inspector will look for traces of the shortcomings in the cash account, the drawings account, and any suspense account in the private ledger. A copy of the accountant's cash and bank reconciliation, and the trial balance may also be helpful to him.

Whether there is a cash surplus or a deficiency, it will be clear to the Inspector that the business records are neither complete nor accurate. The onus for showing that any assessment made by the Inspector in such cases is excessive, passes to the taxpayer. The taxpayer is then in the impossible position of trying to sustain the accuracy of the level of profit returned by reference to generalisations regarding profit rates and wastage. Though not a happy situation to be in, it is entirely the taxpayer's own fault. The accountant should have warned his client about the shortcomings of his records; and if warned, the taxpayer should have taken the advice offered. However, whatever the reason the taxpayer has put himself in a difficult position through a lack of care.

The other general area of the Inspector's initial enquiries concerns estimates. You should be able to establish the amount of your business expenditure by reference to documentary evidence. Minor items that are not capable of exact quantification, such as the cost of the business use of an office in a private house, or the extent of the business use of a car, as against its total use including private use, are areas where estimates are made as a matter of course. What will not be acceptable, for instance, are round sums of cash expenditure attributed to business purchases, but unsupported by any documentary evidence.

Business Records

The Inspector's review of the business records will be concerned with both what they show, and with what they do not show. Normally recurring expenditure that does not appear in the taxpayer's records for a particular week or month is likely to be of considerable interest to the Inspector. He is not intent on showing that you have overstated your profit by omitting genuine business expenses. The Inspector is merely keen to show, by irrefutable evidence, that your records are incomplete and that your accounts are incorrect. If you have met actual business expenses and not recorded them, how can your accounts balance except by understating your business expenditure? You may have met the expenses from your own personal resources, but the business records are still wrong.

It may seem incredible, but taxpayers have been known to submit the 'other' correct set of records to the Inspector, rather than those from which the accounts have been prepared. They may do this by mistake, due to nerves, or because they are confident that the 'other' set of records will withstand close scrutiny as they are indeed correct. However, being a somewhat cautious breed, Inspectors check any records received back against the accounts, so any discrepancies quickly come to light. This procedure does have the advantage of speeding up the enquiry and minimising the accountancy fees involved – and who knows, perhaps there was yet another set of books!

Another general point regarding business records is whether or not sales are recorded *gross*, without deductions of any description. This is to ascertain whether items of business expenditure, and perhaps drawings, have escaped the scrutiny of the accountant by being netted, or set off, against sales. For instance, if you make a sale of £500 and out of the sale money you pay a sub-contractor (who is not an employee) £200 for work connected with the sale, you could simply show a sale of £300, that is £500-£200, in your sales records. Nothing wrong in that, you may say, but the Revenue wish to ensure that your records are both complete and correct. If you are only showing a net sale of £300 you are in fact understating both your sales and your business expenses by £200. Furthermore, nobody has had the opportunity to scrutinise the bona fides of the alleged payment of £200 to the sub-contractor. Suppose the sub-contractor is only prepared to do the work for £200 if there is 'no paper work' involved? What if, when approached by the Revenue, he denies all knowledge of the transaction or claims that he only received £150? You will appreciate that, as the onus of proof passes in such instances to the taxpayer, he is likely to be saddled with paying tax on the whole £500, and not just the £300 included in his accounts. So far as the Inspector is concerned the business sale is £500 and only *verifiable* business expenses may be allowed as a deduction against that figure.

The Inspector may have already looked at the PAYE records, and attempted to reconcile the figures shown with the charge in the accounts for wages. He will also, no doubt, have looked at the declaration made on the form P35 concerning employees to whom PAYE is not considered to be applicable. A supplementary return may have been requested setting out details of the names and addresses of the persons involved, and the respective amounts paid to each of them. He will bear in mind any apparent inconsistencies between the total amounts returned and the total charge in the accounts. The matter will be noted to take up with the taxpayer during the course of the interview if he is unable to resolve the matter by reference to the wages, and, perhaps, the petty cash book.

Your First Interview

The taxpayer, now suitably apprehensive, is ready to be taken like a lamb to the slaughter, to what is probably his first interview with an Inspector of Taxes. The Inspector and accountant are familiar with the course the interview is likely to take, and are not personally involved in the outcome in the true sense. It will be the taxpayer who has to fund the cost of any additional accountancy fees, and tax bill. Therefore all the pressure is on the taxpayer. He is on unfamiliar ground, and in all probability he has not done his homework. He is unlikely to have carried out his own review of his records to see what, if anything, is obviously wrong with them. He may now regret passing through the business the invoice for his hi-fi, or boat, or golf gear, but he is stuck with it. He will almost certainly not have carried out a private side review, or attempted to prepare even rough capital, income, and expenditure statements to see what, if anything, is likely to have to be accounted for to the Inspector.

The taxpayer may be painfully aware of the detailed planning application he made to extend his property, and also know that it would be embarrassing and expensive to have to explain where the money came from to finance the work involved. It may also upset the friends who carried out the work at a special rate 'for cash'. Then there was the cost of the additional furniture, and furnishings, not to mention the exotic holiday unhappily documented by the entry and exit stamps in his passport. The worry is partly the uncertainty: how much does the Inspector know about his business; what is it that has sparked off the present enquiry; is it something he has done; is it because of information from an outside source; is the information in the Inspector's hands even correct? The Inspector will never satisfy his curiosity on the matter although it may be possible to make an informed guess as the enquiry continues. It may be that the taxpayer will never learn the root cause of his problems with the Revenue. The Inspector may be too embarrassed to admit that the information slip had been put in the wrong file!

It is on occasions like this that conscience, or more likely fear of getting caught, makes cowards of us all. The ambience created in Revenue offices by official decor, is unlikely to lift the spirits. It has been explained to me that any exhibition of comfort, let alone luxury, in the offices of a department concerned with levying taxes would be adding visible insult to the financial injury being suffered, so in deference to the taxpayers, the Revenue buildings are generally drab and austere. The rooms occupied by the Inspectors are small and sparsely furnished, although with a new egalitarian spirit each may be fully carpeted – you can no longer judge the grade of the officer you are visiting by the presence, size, or absence of a carpet. However, some indication may be gained from the Inspector's bookcase: if he has a full set of tax case volumes, he is likely to be a fully trained Inspector. If you are seeing the person whose name appears on your tax returns, you have the dubious honour of meeting the District Inspector and any complaints about his or her conduct will have to be addressed to the Regional Office.

The walls of the offices, or cubicles, are paper thin and afford little real privacy. The staff that you will see are career civil servants of varying lengths of service and experience. They tend to be essentially practical people who are perhaps a little cynical after dealing with taxpayers, people of all different types and abilities, but who have one common aim – to lead them up the garden path. They are not normally emotional about their duties, but they may be goaded into taking a closer interest in some enquiries than in others. The more experienced investigators will be capable of dealing with investigations with almost effortless professionalism. It is sensible, therefore, to afford the investigator the respect and consideration that he or she warrants. After all, it is the invetigator who has to be satisfied that the enquiry can be terminated on terms acceptable to you both, if the matter is not to follow the contentious route to the Commissioners. The Inspector has no personal interest in you. His concern is to turn the investigation into a settlement statistic to figure on his annual report, and to move on to the next investigation. So he will be more concerned with getting a reasonable result than in extracting the last drop of your blood.

The initial introductions between the Inspector, the accountant, and the taxpayer will be correct, if not friendly. The accountant and Inspector may already be well known to one another from earlier professional and perhaps social contact. The Inspector will be intent on establishing an informal, business-like relationship with the taxpayer, leaving the accountant, who might become something of a hindrance to the Inspector, on the sidelines. The last thing that the Inspector wants is for the taxpayer to feel inhibited. The more freely the taxpayer can be persuaded to talk, and the more confident he becomes, the more likely he is to let something slip that can lead the Inspector to a successful conclusion of his investigation.

During the course of the interview, the Inspector may use anecdotal illustrations to make his point. For example, he may relate the whimsical tale of the taxpayer who, when questioned about the unbanked cash he held, declared that in the shoe box but omitted to mention the money in the trunk in the loft. The Inspector may follow such a story by emphasising that he wants complete details of *all* unbanked cash held by a taxpayer, from whatever source and wherever kept – even if it is merely being held for a third party. The point of this rigmarole is to make the thrust of the Inspector's questions clear beyond all possible misinterpretation. The combination of the story, the Inspector's questions and the taxpayer's replies is meant to pin the taxpayer down to a position from which he cannot shift later without losing all credibility as a witness. Similarly uncompromising devices will be used in other areas of the enquiry. Therefore the taxpayer will be asked about *all* his bank accounts, of any description: current or deposit, held in the UK or overseas, in his own name or in joint names or under a name of convenience, to ensure that the taxpayer is under no illusion as to what is required.

Once the interview with the taxpayer and the review of the business records have been completed, the Inspector is in a much better position to evaluate the case, and to decide on how far he needs to delve to establish the broad level of understated income and the period involved. His subsequent letters, therefore, are likely to be concerned with the adjustments appropriate to settle the case. If you have claimed to have received money from non-taxable sources, hard evidence in support of those claims will be sought and evaluated. Your demeanour at the interview will be important when the Inspector is evaluating these unsubstantiated claims since he will not only be weighing up the evidence and deciding, on balance, whether or not your account is likely to be true, but also he will be considering what sort of impression you are likely to make as a witness before the Commissioners should the investigation go that far. If he thinks that you will come across as a credible witness and may convince the Commissioners, he will probably reserve his position on the matter, so that the pressure remains on the taxpayer. The item may be used later as a bargaining counter, in negotiating the overall level of additions. Even though he will have effectively decided to accept the story, he is likely to keep the matter open just in case the enquiry goes sour and he needs to use it in a trade-off. The Inspector must also consider how his acceptance of your story may be viewed by his senior officers. Will they think he has gone 'soft' or has been too easily convinced by a highly improbable story? The Inspector may be caught between the desire to settle the case and the need to make the investigation look good. An arrangement may be worked out that will be acceptable to the taxpayer and also may be presented by the investigator as a resounding success. It is for this reason that negotiations are best dealt with at the sensitive stage by the accountant and the Inspector alone, perhaps after a telephone call to establish the lay of the land. However, things can go badly wrong if your accountant misunderstands the degree of latitude he has to negotiate a settlement and later has to renege on an agreement made with the Inspector because the terms are unacceptable to you. If you have any doubts about the matter you will have to insist on being present during any discussions. However, a note of warning: maintain a cool approach in any meeting and remember when renegotiating figures that the original sum will only have been reached after hard bargaining between the Inspector and your accountant.

Let us go back a stage and look once again at the Inspector's request for information, access to business and private records, and an interview. The Inspector should be prepared to accept your accounts, returns and computations unless he has reason to believe that they do not set out your income correctly and fully, in accordance with the Taxation Acts. The 'accounts' referred to here are an integral part of your income tax return.

Prior to FA1990 Sections 90 and 91, it was open to argument that an Inspector had no right to *demand* a set of accounts in support of a figure of income, computed in accordance with the terms of the Income and Corporation Tax Acts, unless he had reason not to be satisfied with the figure of profit returned, based on some particular evidence. In this context it should be borne in mind that the Inspector does not have the power to be irrationally or perversely dissatisfied. There must be a logical demonstrable reason for his dissatisfaction. The amendment of the return sections by Sections 90 and 91 FA1990 however, now give the Inspector the power to *require* different information, accounts and statements, for different periods, or in relation to different descriptions of sources of income, and to deliver such accounts and statements with the tax return.

The form in which the accounts are submitted to the Revenue is entirely up to the taxpayer as their layout and requirements are not specified in the Taxes Acts. The development of the standard form adopted for the presentation of accounts has largely been dictated by the acountancy profession, a profession which largely owes its existence to the demands of the Revenue. A major industry has developed concerned with accountancy standards and the measurement of profits for certain industries, with the accountancy profession becoming the unelected representatives of taxpayers. This has come about because of the lack of any specific guidance in the Taxes Acts as to how the full profits or gains from any particular activities are to be arrived at. The Courts have had to rely on the professional evidence of accountants to decide what is and is not acceptable for accountancy purposes to arrive at the profit, subject to any specific items disallowed under the provisions of the Taxes Act. A pragmatic solution to a difficult problem. The outcome has been that nearly all business people now use an accountant to produce accounts, basically for the benefit of the Revenue. The Board is secure in the knowledge that a substantial part of the work of vetting taxpayers' accounts rests with the accountancy profession – who are being employed by the taxpayers at no cost to the Board. If the profitability of any enterprise is challenged by the Revenue, unorthodox accounts, prepared by an accountant who does not belong to a recognised association, are unlikely to be acceptable to any body of Commissioners as evidence of the true profits of the enterprise. It is the possibility of such a challenge that has led to the convention of submitting certified accounts annually to the Revenue, the certification being done predominantly by members of the main recognised societies of accountants.

If, then, the Inspector states he is not satisfied with your accounts and/or income tax returns, he should be pressed to explain precisely what the cause of his dissatisfaction is. Reasonable requests for access to business records can be complied with, the inspection of the records taking place in the accountant's office, where the accountant can assist the Inspector in resolving any queries. The Inspector should not be allowed to undertake a general fishing expedition into the private records; the precise relevance of the records to his enquiries should be established. Do not attempt to obstruct the Inspector in carrying out his legitimate duties, but do insist on your own rights to consideration and privacy. You should not be expected to incur additional expenditure without due cause. After all, the Inspector's enquiry may be based on incorrect or misleading information supplied by a third party.

The First Capital Settlement

If after consideration of the points made by the Inspector your accountant advises you that there is a *prima facie* case to answer, you and/or your accountant should draw up basic capital, income and expenditure statements and discuss the results. If it emerges from the statements that unexplained income does exist, it is then time to advise the Inspector of the position, and to extend the statements to a period when your affairs can be fully and satisfactorily explained. Your accountant should also be involved in making any adjustments necessary to the book-keeping procedures followed, and any tightening up of the prime records to ensure that no further leakage can occur. Then, with your authority, he may write to the Inspector advising him of the position.

The review may indicate that substantial amounts of business money have not gone through the accounts and have found their way into private bank accounts, or have been utilised in meeting private expenditure. Clearly, if this is the case, you may be in some jeopardy and expert advice should perhaps be sought. You will hardly be ignorant of the position, but may be surprised – if not dismayed – by the amounts that become visible when the statements are drawn up.

If the method of extraction has involved the falsification of business records or collusion with other taxpayers to conspire to defraud the Revenue, criminal charges could be involved and a solicitor should be consulted – and any advice given, followed.

In the normal course of events the mere size or level of extractions does not affect the Revenue's procedure of seeking to negotiate a monetary settlement. However, if you present the Inspector with hard documentary evidence that will unequivocally support a criminal prosecution, and follow it up with a full and frank confession after being given a formal warning in accordance with the Judges' Rules at the Inspector's interview, then you must expect the logical conclusion to follow. Easy prosecutions in tax cases are not common but they are welcome and the publicity surrounding a successful Revenue prosecution assists the Revenue in its bread and butter enquiries. It encourages others to be more prepared to enter into monetary settlements, being only too pleased that they are not also being prosecuted.

Returning to the Inspector's request for an interview, the Taxation Acts do not require a taxpayer to attend the tax office for any purpose. There is also no requirement, if you choose to go voluntarily, for you to answer any questions that the Inspector chooses to ask. You may attend the Inspector's office with your accountant, and only answer any questions your accountant, as your professional adviser, feels to be relevant, appropriate and suitable to be answered without prior, private consultation. Such a response may annoy the Inspector and so strengthen his resolve to get to the bottom of the case that you do yourself positive harm. However, the point to note is that the Inspector's powers are limited, and he must be suitably circumspect in the application of the more draconian sections of the Tax Acts. Your accountant should be expected to give you positive advice and assistance at any interview. All too often accountants attend interviews with clients and just wait to see what the Inspector will do. When the taxpayer has made a mess of the interview, and the Inspector has asked the taxpayer all the questions that the accountant wanted the answers to, but did not like to ask, the accountant can resume the normal duties of his practice by carrying out the requirements of the Inspector – at the taxpayer's expense.

You may feel that I have overstated the situation and that the scenario outlined could never happen to you. I can only suggest that you consult others who have had first hand experience of a Revenue investigation before you reach a firm conclusion on the matter.

Gross Profit Rates

The Inspector's enquiries will seek to establish that your books and records are incorrect or incomplete. Once this has been established the claim will be made that, because of the errors or omissions discovered, the records are unreliable. The Inspector is then faced with putting forward alternative profit figures. This will normally be done by looking at the stock figures at the beginning and end of the year, plus the purchases, and trying to establish a theoretically realistic profit, based on the prices that could be charged for the items sold, or the services rendered. This can be done for retail shops, etc. by looking at the mark-up normally added to the purchase price of various classes of stock and ascertaining the profit mix of the items sold: for instance, 40 per cent with a 15 per cent mark up; 30 per cent with a 45 per cent mark up, and so on. The Revenue have produced copies of business notes applicable to various businesses which are available to the general public. If you are making the 'approved' level of gross profit on sales the Inspector may have some difficulty in arguing that a larger profit should have been made.

Some taxpayers are well aware of the gross profit rate percentage argument and have accordingly suppressed some purchases, excluding them from their books, records and accounts. This may at first seem a little strange; business people are not well known for understating business expenditure. The point is, however, that if you do not have goods to sell you cannot make any profit. So purchases are understated, and the sales in respect of the omitted purchases are also excluded from the business records. The result is that the gross profit rate percentage made by the business will be unaffected by the sales money that has been extracted. The Inspector is aware of this practice, and many others, that have been used to 'doctor' business records and accounts. What the Inspector needs is an entirely independent way to cross-check the results shown by the business accounts and for this he may use the private side review.

Private Expenditure

The Inspector will seek to identify any way in which he can attempt to reconstruct your pattern and level of private expenditure. All drawings from the business, both recorded and unrecorded, will be reflected in what you have spent or saved (*see* Chapter 2).

The Inspector will approach the enquiry in a fragmented way but will look at the business and private records together, comparatively. He is trying to show:

- that the business has the actual earning potential he is attributing to it;
- that you have access, and the ability to make the extractions as alleged by him;
- that you have actually utilised the money extracted to meet private expenditure, or to make investments and savings.

Each of these items is to some extent interdependent. If the Inspector can demonstrate that the business could have made more money, that is not sufficient unless he can also show that you had physical access to business money and could bypass the records. In addition he must also show that each of those events actually occurred by pointing to how you disposed of your ill-gotten gains. It is for this reason that the Inspector will wish to scrutinise your private records, seeking to establish that you have a life-style and level of expenditure that could not be supported by the level of profit and drawings you have recorded in your books, records and accounts.

If the private side expenditure figures *do* show a level of income way above that which the business is capable of supporting, the Inspector will not waste time or energy trying to account for the phenomenon; he will treat the full amount as additional extracted profit, and leave you to account for it. It will be difficult to support claims to have received gifts from friends and other non-taxable sources, and corroborative evidence will be asked for. It may be possible to persuade some bodies of Commissioners that explanations relating to other, rather improbable, non-taxable sources might have some credence: for example, family money and valuables smuggled in from abroad, or family jewellery, other goods and chattels sold in the UK. However, the Inspector would wish to see at least good circumstantial evidence in support of such transactions – some evidence of the steps taken to sell the items at least.

4 The Business Review

The Inspector will be interested in the precise nature and extent of the duties of the proprietors, partners, or directors. He will aim to know the physical day-to-day trading activities and specifically who does what, his concern being to show that there are opportunities for the extraction of monies from the business. To this end the Inspector may go through your daily procedure for recording sales and the receipt of monies, and the payment of bills and wages. The nature and extent of the prime records such as invoices or till rolls, who inputs the information and when, the arrangements for writing up the business records and the particular prime records from which the figures are taken are all areas likely to receive attention. The type of work carried out by the accountant on the business records prior to producing your accounts also may be explored.

The Takings

A number of businesses use standard business transaction summary books as an easy way to keep records that are convenient for their accountants and hopefully reduce the cost of preparing their accounts. The accountant may well not check the arithmetic of the weekly cash and bank summaries, relying on an overall view produced from the bank account entries and the total annual figures for the cash account. The figures for opening and closing cash in hand may not be actual figures resulting from a count of the cash on the appropriate days but merely computed figures arising from the other entries in the daily/weekly business records. If the accountant has not checked these items the Inspector may well consider it worthwhile carrying out test checks. Spot checks over various periods within the period of the account may reveal a negative cash position. Such discrepancies may be swept up into an annual cash account and disappear without trace but, as it is not physically possible to have a negative cash position, the Inspector may rely on such evidence to support a claim that your business records are incomplete and inaccurate.

Attention is likely to be paid to the levels of turnover achieved. Turnover may vary considerably over a year as the trade may be seasonal, producing marked fluctuations. The Inspector will try to make sense of the variations in the recorded sales figures by reference to information in the business records regarding purchases, wages, fuel expenses etc., using his personal knowledge of local circumstances to evaluate them. Inspectors naturally build up a local expertise from seeing large numbers of accounts for the area covered by the district and will keep an eye open for details that do not ring true. Clumsy attempts to trim takings towards year ends or at peak periods of business are likely to be spotted.

Purchases
Careless book-keeping can also give rise to problems on the purchases side. It is not unknown for some regularly recurring payments to be omitted from records because the relevant invoices are settled in cash direct from takings and the paperwork not passed on to the person writing up the business records. If proper daily balanced cash records are being kept, such errors would immediately come to light if the takings are being recorded gross. However, when business records are written up some time after the events in question, the chances are that balancing figures will be adopted to produce a balanced cash account and the Inspector will again be able to show that the business records are incomplete and inaccurate. The Inspector's interest may be aroused by adjustments made during the course of a year to cover errors discovered by the book-keeper or proprietor. Again questions will be directed to establishing the nature and extent of the weaknesses in the business records that gave rise to the errors.

The purchase invoices may be examined in some detail as it is not uncommon to discover very obvious private items that have not been charged to drawings. The examination may extend to checking the cash and carry invoice codes to identify private expenditure items. If the Inspector can show that you have charged private expenditure against business receipts so that business profits have been understated, he can claim that you have been guilty of neglect and have failed to return the full and correct profit of the business. Your neglect is that you have not taken the necessary steps to eliminate your private expenditure from the amounts charged as business expenses. In addition, the purchases will be examined to identify fictitious or inflated items. Suppliers may have provided inflated false invoices. To check for this the Inspector may obtain the cancelled cheques from your bank with a view to identifying items not made out to the payees described on the cheque book counterfoil and in the cash book. In such transactions the money is often drawn as cash rather than actually being paid to the 'supplier'. If the invoice is inflated, however, the money is likely to find its way back to the business in the form of a cash discount.

Purchase and stock figures may be analysed so that the throughput of each classification of stock is broadly identified. The mark-up adopted to each class of stock can then be applied to reconstruct the anticipated sales figure. If there is a substantial discrepancy between the anticipated and actual sales figures recorded, an explanation will be sought.

Discounts and commissions are another area that may well come under scrutiny. Discounts on business purchases can be very substantial and restrictions have been placed on discounts given in particular trades. The practice of showing only part of the full discount on the invoice, the balance being paid in cash, is known to the Revenue as is the temptation to taxpayers to pocket the additional discount rather than set it off against the purchases. The person paying the commission will wish to claim the charge against business profits so the payment of the cash will be documented in his or her records. A simple cross check may reveal the full discount involved. Investigation cases may arise from information supplied by other offices of the Revenue involved in an examination of the accounts of the payer – and details of cash payments made extracted from the payer's records may find their way into the files of the recipients.

Peripheral activities of the trade may well be known to the Inspector and, as part of his check of the business records, he may seek to verify that all sources of income have been properly recorded in the business books. The sub-letting of part of the business premises for instance may be revealed by an inspection of the premises or by reference to the voter's list, if residential occupation is involved.

Drawings

Drawings are an obvious area for enquiry. The first thing to establish is that the proprietors are at least claiming to record gross takings, that is before the deduction of any drawings or 'wife's wages'/housekeeping. The make up of the drawings account should normally disclose regular weekly/monthly drawings plus specific cheque items such as NIC and tax payments. In some instances drawings are by transfer to a private bank account or there could be a mixture of such transfers and cash drawings directly from the business. Whatever method or mixture of methods for drawing money from the business is adopted the Inspector will aim to evaluate whether you have sufficient recorded means to meet your private requirements. If there is any shortfall he will assume, in the absence of any satisfactory explanation, that the additional funds necessary to meet your needs have come from the business as unrecorded drawings.

Capital Introduced

If monies have been introduced into the business from sources outside the business, verification of the sources involved will be sought. Loans or gifts from relatives or friends will be viewed with some suspicion and may result in the taxation affairs of the payer coming under scrutiny, to check whether the sum advanced is from sources known to the Revenue. Similarly monies introduced from betting winnings or the sale of household assets are likely to be treated with some scepticism and proof of the transactions requested.

5 Capital Statements

The stage has now been set. The Inspector has made his challenge, interviewed the taxpayer, and examined the business records. If, as is usually the case, he has not been satisfied by what he has seen, the investigation will proceed along well worn paths, and may involve expensive correspondence covering a period of years. The process aims to assemble evidence to show that profits have been understated and to quantify the understatement. By this point the Inspector will have given consideration to the number of years for which the profits may have been understated. If he is satisfied that he has 'made a discovery' (in accordance with Section 29(3) TMA1970) that profits have been understated he may make additional assessments.

Under the provisions of Section 36 of the TMA1970 the Inspector may, for the purpose of making good to the Crown a loss of tax attributable to fraudulent or negligent conduct, on the part of the taxpayer or a person acting on his behalf, make assessments on any person at any time not later than 20 years after the end of the chargeable period to which the assessment relates.

If the person in default carried on a trade in partnership with other individuals, assessments may be made on the partners as well.

The provisions of Section 36 now also apply to companies. These new provisions were enacted by Section 149 FA1989 and only apply for the years of assessment 1983/4 onwards and for the accounting periods ending after 31st March 1983. Prior to this the earlier form of Section 36 applies.

The S88 Interest Charge

The Inspector will advise you in advance why he is making further or additional assessments. He will claim that they are for the purpose of recovering any tax that may have been lost due to failures or errors on your part. These include: failure to give notice or make a return; failure to produce or furnish a document, or other information required by, or under the Taxes Acts; and delivering information, a return, an account, or other document to the Revenue which contains an error. The technical reason for supplying this information is to establish in writing the precise purpose for which the assessments are being made. Assessments made for the purposes set out above may carry interest under Section 88 TMA1970. Under the provisions of that section, where an assessment has been made for the purpose of making good to the Crown a loss of tax wholly or partly attributable to a failure on the part of the taxpayer, the tax charged by the assessment (or such part of it as corresponds to the part so attributable) will be liable to carry interest.

The notice of determination will show:

● the date of issue;
● the amount of tax carrying interest and the assessments concerned;
● the date on which for Section 88 purposes the tax ought to have been paid;
● the time limit for making appeals against the determination.

Once the notice of determination has been served and the time limit for making an appeal has expired, the determination cannot be varied. The determination may be made within six years after the end of the chargeable period for which the tax is charged, or within three years after the date of the final determination of the tax.

Appeals against such determinations should be made to the Commissioners who, if it appears to them that the tax carries no interest under Section 88 may set aside the determination. If the determination appears to them to be correct they must confirm it; if incorrect, they may revise the amount of the tax or the date on which the tax ought to have been paid. The time when the tax ought to have been paid is defined in Section 88(5) and for income tax it is 1 January in the year of assessment for which the tax is charged. If the tax would have been payable in two instalments, the relevant dates are 1 January and 1 July. The date for capital gains tax is 1 December in the year of assessment following the year for which the tax is charged. Corporation tax follows the original due dates that would have applied if the assessments had been made at the proper times for each of the accounting periods concerned.

The rate of interest eligible under Section 88 has varied from year to year broadly in line with changes in the bank rate or base rate. The prescribed rates are set out in Section 89 TMA1970. The idea behind the interest charge is not to impose a penalty as such but merely to enable the Board to obtain commercial restitution for the loss of the use of the money from its original due date to the time of payment. A new subparagraph (7) has been added to Section 88 that includes in relation to anything required to be done at a particular time or within a particular period, a reference to a failure to do it at that time or within that period; and the normal let-out clause in Section 118(2) does not apply. Section

Capital Statements

118(2) effectively allowed any failure to be remedied within such further time as the Board, Commissioners or officer allowed. It also deemed the taxpayer not to have failed to do anything required to be done, if he did it without unreasonable delay after his reasonable excuse for the failure had ceased.

You should by now be aware of the legal significance of the steps that the Inspector is taking against you, and what costs could be involved if the assessments made are determined by the Commissioners and any determination under Section 88 confirmed. The Inspector has moved the investigation forward.

You must realize the seriousness of your position. The Inspector is asserting that he has made a discovery that income has not been assessed or that an assessment is, or has become, insufficient. The assessments are made for the purpose of 'making good to the Crown a loss of tax wholly or partly attributable to the fraudulent or negligent conduct' of you and/or your company. In the case of a company, alternative assessments may be made on you as a director under the provisions of Schedule E as well as on your company under the corporation tax provisions. Assessments may also be made on the company under the provisions of Section 419 ICTA1988 if it is considered that as the result of your alleged extractions you may have an overdrawn balance on your current and/or loan account. It will be small comfort to you to learn that the Revenue will not seek to assess you under Schedule E under the provisions of Section 160 ICTA 1988 in respect of beneficial loans if Section 419 assessments are made for the purpose of recovering tax lost. I will deal with company matters separately (*see* Chapter 10).

When the assessments descend upon you, the full horror of your situation will become apparent. The Inspector's estimates may seem excessive – even fanciful – but do not be deceived. The Inspector will have prepared a rational argument in support of his figures and if he can establish a prima facie case of a loss of tax due to fraudulent or negligent conduct, the onus is upon you to *show* that the assessments are excessive, otherwise they will stand.

Fight or Flight?

The first consideration is a realistic appraisal of your situation and the evidence that has been assembled in support of the Inspector's assessments. You will know the truth of the matter even if nobody else does and you will have to make a very hard decision. Once you have totalled the tax bill involved and obtained details of the Section 88 interest and the penalties situation and your accountant has given you some idea of the total bill likely to be involved, the initial reaction is normally to fight the Inspector's absurd assessments. If this is what you decide to

45

do, further protracted correspondence may follow, covering a period of years. The correspondence will seek explanations and verifications of the sources of monies credited to bank, building society, or savings accounts. If previously undisclosed accounts and transactions emerge, they will be explored in depth and efforts will be made to establish the amount of the cash needed to support your life-style. You may find that the truth hangs together rather well whereas lies or half-truths may lead you to dig a deeper hole for yourself. You may discover that the initial interview with the Inspector and the agreed interview notes considerably restrict your room to manoeuvre. Probably, at the time of the interview you had not prepared an overall view of your affairs over the previous six years and, therefore, were unprepared for the Inspector's carefully prepared and detailed questions. When faced with the need to explain a specific transaction or cash flow position, you may have responded 'off the top of your head' with a spurious explanation which you have had to change or even abandon later in the interview or investigation. Obviously this sort of situation is what the Inspector was aiming for. However, had a full review of your affairs been carried out before the interview, giving you the opportunity to consider carefully the matters in question, your position may have been less fraught. In that situation you would have known what needed to be accounted for and when, and have been prepared to clarify any apparent inconsistencies in your account of events.

Guilty knowledge may mean that you (and other taxpayers) experience considerable stress when attending the tax office and these psychological pressures may muddle your thinking. You should appreciate also that a skilled investigator may deliberately use those pressures to obtain an admission of irregularities. The Inspector's reiteration of questions about a particular aspect of your affairs, highlighting any lack of conviction or weakness in your account, can be a very effective technique. The circumstantial evidence undermining your claims builds up, pressurising and discouraging you. At this stage the Inspector may deliver a further shock, such as introducing a statement from an informer or business associate that you knew nothing about. At this point you may be very vulnerable, perhaps making a statement that you deeply regret later. If only through the popular media, everyone is aware of various interrogation techniques and how the outcome of interviews can vary depending on the knowledge and skill of the interviewee. The Inspector of Taxes investigating your financial affairs will use techniques similar to those employed by police and customs officers, thus you should treat the tax interview with suitable respect. Be prepared and keep calm, after all if things do not go well, you could end up in court.

The police officer's enquiries normally begin in response to a reported crime and his concern is with finding the culprit. The Tax Inspector, however, may start his enquiry with only a suspicion that an offence has been committed, though he may also be acting on specific information received. Needless to say, he will not disclose the extent of his information, to prevent you limiting your disclosure to that particular item. If anything is wrong, all your affairs will be gone through in detail.

You may speculate about the cause of the Inspector's dissatisfaction with your affairs. You may try to reconstruct the information that you know the Inspector holds from correspondence, returns and accounts, and also consider what horrors could have emerged from other sources. Perhaps more to the point, you may consider alternative ways in which you could have conducted your affairs if you had any inkling in advance of what a Revenue investigation involves. At this stage it is too late to discover that the best solution is not to be in your present predicament.

Hard or Circumstantial Evidence?

The conduct and outcome of the investigation will depend on the evidence obtained during the course of the enquiry. That evidence will consist of your business and private records, your income tax returns and accounts, and the statements that have been made by you or on your behalf over the years and during the course of the enquiry. An adjunct to this evidence may be information from a third party, perhaps from their business records. Hard direct evidence may be thin and it may be possible to successfully deny some inferences drawn, or statements made by third parties. There is a divide between the evidence required for a criminal prosecution, which must be 'beyond reasonable doubt', and that necessary for a civil action, the test of which being the 'balance of probabilities'. A direct confession clearly places you in the 'beyond reasonable doubt' position, while a denial in the face of overwhelming circumstantial evidence leaves you caught by the 'balance of probabilities'.

A further consideration is the complexity of the transactions involved and the documentary evidence necessary to establish each step in those transactions 'beyond reasonable doubt'. A break in the full chain of evidence necessary to establish the complete transaction will mean that the evidence fails the stringent criminal test. It is precisely for this reason that documents are 'lost' or destroyed, or that transactions take place for cash with no documentary evidence.

In considering your position you will need to give thought to who you might call as a witness on your behalf or, alternatively, who the Revenue may call to assist the case against you. If there is something demonstrably wrong with your taxation affairs you should, through your legal adviser, enter into negotiations with the Inspector on a 'without prejudice' basis, giving strict instructions that all correspondence with the Inspector is headed 'without prejudice'. This simple step will prevent the correspondence being either used in evidence at any appeal hearing or referred to directly by the Inspector. This is a technical ploy to keep the Inspector's position as weak as possible right up to the conclusion of the investigation.

The negotiations with the Inspector should be realistic. If you present your capital, income and expenditure statements either in response to a request from the Inspector, or to comply with a Commissioner's precept, you should ensure that the statements of assets and liabilities are complete and that the schedules of private expenditure are capable of being defended, if necessary before the Commissioners.

The Part Played by Capital Statements

The construction of the capital, income and expenditure statements is such that the amount required to balance the income plus or minus the capital decrease or increase in the year equals the total private expenditure. In investigation cases it is normally found that the declared income has to be increased by the amount of the extractions made from the business in order to produce an amount which is capable of meeting private expenditure. It is often at this stage that past misdeeds are compounded by efforts to understate or minimise private expenditure to a ridiculous degree, in an attempt to get away with an inadequate figure for the extractions made. If you go out of your way to convince the Inspector that you have no intention of making a complete disclosure he will react by going over all the details in the cash and bank reconciliations on the private side to prove that you are still being less than honest and forthcoming. It will sour the negotiations and make a reasonable conclusion of the investigation difficult.

The Inspector will have dealt with your level of private expenditure in broad terms at the opening interview. It is rare for anybody to be able to account for how they spend the money used for private expenses. It is easier to establish the amount actually drawn over a specific period and to ask if the amounts involved are representative. Any exceptional items of expenditure may be explained by the taxpayer.

In relation to cash expenditure it is reasonable to assume that when cash is drawn, that amount has been virtually expended by the time the next amount is drawn in cash. In this way there may be a particular period in the year when cash expenditure for a period of weeks is exceptionally high. The Inspector will argue with some force that it was not that the expenditure was high but that, for some reason or another, your extractions from the business were exceptionally low for that period. Clearly there is room for negotiation in such circumstances, but you are in a stronger position if the figures you are putting forward look reasonable in the context of the actual cash drawings.

The retail price index can be used by the Revenue to extrapolate figures backwards and forwards over the years of the enquiry when relevant. The Inspector will naturally choose the drawings for the highest period to adopt as his norm. The cash drawings will be looked at in conjunction with the private expenditure met from cheque drawings. Some care is taken in the examination of bank accounts to ensure that all four quarters of standing bills such as gas, electricity, and telephone are shown. The same position arises concerning mortgage payments, school fees, and so on. Any missing items will be taken as additional cash expenditure in addition to the weekly/monthly general house-keeping figure. Credit card accounts may be examined to ensure that all credits to the accounts have been shown in the bank accounts or dealt with in the cash account.

Holiday expenditure will receive similar consideration. For instance the cost of a holiday may appear in the bank account or a credit card account without any apparent provision for traveller's cheques and foreign currency, or sterling if the holiday is in the UK. These items will all be swept up into the cash account. If it is established that holidays are taken abroad in property of any description owned by the taxpayer, the Inspector will wish to ensure that the full cost of financing the purchase of the assets has been properly dealt with in the statements. In addition the possibility of foreign bank accounts and the letting of the premises will be discussed at some length. No doubt in the future there will be greater use of the exchange of information provisions contained in double taxation agreements entered into by various countries with the UK. It is clear that, because of the trafficking in drugs and the attempts to launder the proceeds of those transactions and other crimes, more information concerning the overseas and UK bank accounts used for such transactions may become available to the Revenue. It should be noted that the provisions for the exchange of information between governments are already in place.

If, as the result of your accountant's negotiations with the Inspector, some figures are produced that you could not expect to get reduced if you took the matter on appeal to the Commissioners you may authorise your accountant to accept the additional assessments that flow from the agreed figures. The Inspector could not be a party to demanding tax that is not accepted to be due by the taxpayer. However, the taxpayer is not obliged to confess in graphic detail how he took the money and falsified the business records. On the other hand, if the taxpayer continues to deny any irregularities, the Inspector may be forced to take the appeals that are outstanding before the Commissioners for determination. There must be tacit acceptance by the taxpayer that the Revenue can show that there is something wrong with his records, accounts and returns in order to bring the investigation to its settlement stage.

The time and cost involved in reaching the settlement stage may be minimized if you authorise your accountant to carry out a thorough review of your affairs and produce the necessary capital, income and expenditure statements, to withstand the scrutiny of the Inspector. Remember that the Inspector is an employee of a large organisation, subjected to the same pressures and aspirations that are found in commerce. His work is likely to be examined by others seeking to assess his performance and efficiency. Cost-effectiveness is an important consideration for the Revenue so, while he will not wish to have files implying that he has been duped, neither will he wish to appear to have delayed the settlement of an investigation unnecessarily, and wasted valuable time.

If for some reason you and your accountant are not sufficiently persuasive to obtain the Inspector's agreement to figures you feel to be eminently sustainable, you had better make up your mind to ask the Inspector to list the appeals for a contentious hearing by the Commissioners. The open appeals can be settled by the Commissioners after hearing all the relevant evidence.

6 Appeals

The administration of the Income Tax, Corporation Tax, and Capital Gains Tax is under the care and management of the Commissioners of Inland Revenue, known as 'The Board'. It is the Board who appoint Inspectors and Collectors of Taxes to act under the direction of the Board of Inland Renenue. (Section 1 TMA1970). For the purpose of exercising such powers relating to appeals and other matters as are conferred on them by the Taxes Acts there are Commissioners for the general purposes of the Income Tax called General Commissioners. The General Commissioners are appointed by the Lord Chancellor to act for divisions in England and Wales. In Scotland the Secretary of State makes appointments of General Commissioners. (Section 2 TMA1970). The General Commissioners in turn appoint a Clerk and, if considered necessary, an assistant Clerk. The General Commissioners receive no remuneration in respect of their services but their Clerk is paid by the Board of Inland Revenue. (Section 3 TMA1970). The General Commissioners are a lay body comprising of local businessmen and women of standing and they rely on their Clerk, who is normally a qualified solicitor, to advise them on the law. They have no specialist taxation knowledge apart from what they acquire in service as General Commissioners.

You can elect to have your appeal heard by the Special Commissioners who are a stipendiary body who sit in London. Generally, however, it is neither advisable nor cost-effective to have the appeal heard by the Special Commissioners, especially if you and/or your accountant live and work in the provinces. The same procedure for the hearing of appeals applies whether the appeal is heard by the Special Commissioners or the General Commissioners. However, being a stipendiary body and dealing with appeals all the time, Appeals before Special Commissioners are likely to be more formal.

The General and Special Commissioners do not have the power to award costs so you will have to bear the costs of presenting your case to them, whatever the outcome of the hearing. If you go on to the High Court (or Court of Sessions in Scotland) or beyond, the award of costs will normally follow the outcome of the appeal. You could, therefore, be awarded costs in the higher courts, but if you lose you could have costs awarded against you.

In an appeal before the Commissioners the Revenue will normally be represented by the Inspector dealing with the case or by the District Inspector. If the Revenue consider it appropriate, they may be represented by a member of the Inland Revenue's Solicitors' Branch, but this is very unlikely. The taxpayer may represent himself or be represented by Counsel, a solicitor, or his accountant provided he or she is a member of an incorporated society of accountants (Section 50(5) TMA 1970).

Witnesses
'The Commissioners may summon any person (other than the appellant) to appear before them and give evidence, and a witness before the Commissioners may be examined on oath' (Section 52(2) TMA1970). It may seem strange at first sight that the appellant cannot be summoned to give evidence. However, the matter will only come before Commissioners if the taxpayer has appealed against an assessment and the Commissioners may only reduce the assessment if 'it appears to the majority of the Commissioners present at the hearing, by examination of the appellant on oath or affirmation, or by other lawful evidence, that the appellant is overcharged by any assessment, the assessment shall be reduced accordingly, but otherwise every such assessment shall stand good.' (Section 50(6) TMA1970). Therefore, if you appeal against an assessment it is up to you to show by lawful evidence that it is excessive. If you choose to let matters go by default after having appealed against an assessment, at best the assessment will be confirmed by the Commissioners. However, the Inspector may produce evidence to show that the assessment is inadequate, even though the assessment was made by him in the first place. In those circumstances Section 50(7) TMA1970 provides that 'if on any appeal it appears to the Commissioners that the person assessed ought to be charged in an amount exceeding the amount contained in the assessment, the assessment shall be increased accordingly.' It is, therefore, incumbent on you to appear before the Commissioners and to ensure that all lawful evidence available to support your case is produced.

You will note that a person 'confidentially employed in the affairs of the appellant' cannot be required to give evidence. He may refuse to be sworn or to answer any question to which he objects. Nevertheless, such a person may be summoned by the Commissioners to give evidence and if he does not appear before them 'shall incur a penalty not exceeding £50'. There is nothing to stop such a person appearing and then refusing to be sworn or to answer any question to which he objects. However, the Commissioners are likely to take note of the Inspector's questions that the witness declines to answer. On such occasions silence may be quite eloquent.

The Commissioners may examine witnesses on oath and the provisions of the Perjury Act apply. Giving false evidence under oath is a very serious matter, constituting a criminal offence in its own right. It is better to admit to having no recollection of events, if that is indeed the case, than to supply false or incorrect information.

The appeal hearing will come at the end of the Revenue investigation because agreement cannot be reached over the size of the assessments or because there is a denial of any culpability in respect of any loss of tax alleged by the Revenue to be involved. However, if the Revenue is to mount a criminal prosecution there will be no hearing of the appeal by the Commissioners to determine the amount of the assessments. The criminal charge will take precedence and the matter will go to the Magistrates Court for committal proceedings.

The Revenue will advise the Clerk to the Commissioners of the appeals that are to be determined. The Revenue will also give the Clerk some idea of the time likely to be needed for the case to be heard, so that the Commissioners can ensure that they will be available to hear all the evidence and legal arguments from the Revenue and the appellant. The Clerk will then give notice of the date, time, and place for the hearing of the appeal to the appellant and the Revenue. It is preferable to tell the Inspector and the Clerk, prior to any appeal hearing date being set, of dates that you or your advisers would wish to avoid. This should avert any conflict with the Commissioners prior to the hearing concerning their domestic arrangements.

The Taxpayer's Brief

Before the arrangements for an appeal hearing begin you should give serious consideration to the strengths and weaknesses of your case, the evidence that will need to be adduced, and the witnesses, if any, that will have to be called. You may find it helpful to prepare a full statement of precisely what you wish to say to the Commissioners. The best way to express yourself will emerge and the phraseology that might suggest unwelcome aspects of your evidence to the Commissioners can be avoided. You must provide the evidence that is necessary to sustain your contentions. If you wish to establish that you have received monies from non-taxable sources such as gifts, bequests, loans, betting winnings, and so on then you need to think in realistic terms of the evidence that may be produced. To have reached the stage of an appeal hearing means that you will have already put your claims to the Inspector and had them rejected. He will no doubt have used the wording of the Act in stating that he is not satisfied that the money came from non-taxable sources.

There is no doubt that either during the course of correspondence or at an interview, in both written and verbal representations, you have failed to impress the Inspector with the strength of your case. Clearly if there is good documentary evidence from the donor's bank account and perhaps a statement from the payer verifying the gift, bequest, or loan, you will have no difficulty in convincing the Inspector that he cannot maintain his 'not satisfied' stance. Difficulties normally arise when the money is not clearly identifiable in the donor's accounts or is in cash that, for one reason or another, has been kept deliberately undocumented. Perhaps the payer has died, or is resident abroad, or is otherwise uncooperative. In such circumstances you are thrown back on circumstantial evidence. You should consider each transaction in depth and the facts that may assist you may become apparent. Details of the reason for the money passing to you at that particular time, the arrangements made to hand it over, and the actual place where the money was passed over together with a list of the other people present will give you a starting point. Then try to remember what clothing you and the payer were wearing, where you went for meals, the size and nature of the parcel or container in which the cash was kept before you received it and what became of the container or wrapping. Where did you keep the cash after its receipt? Was anybody else aware of your good fortune? If so, who, when, and in what circumstances did they find out? Can they give evidence to assist you?

You will appreciate that if you claim to have returned home one day with a parcel of cash asserting that it came from Uncle Arthur, even if you have a house full of witnesses, they can only give evidence that you produced the money and claimed that it came from Uncle Arthur. Even if Uncle Arthur arrived at your house bringing a parcel of cash and handed it over to you proclaiming that it was a gift to you in front of independent witnesses, that would still not be proof positive that the money did not in fact emanate from your business activities. You must be able to show that Uncle Arthur had the money to give – in his own right – and is not merely recycling your money for your convenience.

Betting Stories
Betting stories are a not uncommon explanation for the source of monies in Revenue investigation cases and bookmakers have been known to collude with taxpayers in providing evidence of winning bets. If a bookmaker wishes to depress his recorded profits, the introduction of fictitious bets showing punters winning money from him provides a convenient way of achieving the objective. The bookmaker does not actually part with any money and will normally be charging to provide the false documentation – say ten per cent of the 'winnings'. If anybody

were to go to such lengths to establish betting winnings they are still not home and dry as the Courts have indicated that it is not sufficient to produce evidence of betting winnings; a full record of all betting activities showing winnings and losses must be produced. In some cases taxpayers have resorted to old records of winning horses and/or dogs to reconstruct a believable record of betting activities. The results produced are normally inaccurate in some detail and can be shown to have been manufactured: to fabricate cast iron stories requires considerable knowledge and expertise. Again, circumstantial evidence is needed to assist such accounts. If on-course betting is involved, are you claiming to have travelled alone or in company? What mode of transport was adopted? Did anybody else see you at the racecourse? Do you have a circle of friends or acquaintances that you meet at the course? Which courses do you attend and why? Can you describe the animals that won the races? What made you decide to back those particular animals? What stakes do you normally place on each race? What decides the size of your bet? Where is the stake money held? How do you deal with stake money and winnings? If you have been involved in successfully beating the bookmakers you will be something of a rarity and the questions posed should give you no difficulty. It is up to you to ensure that the Commissioners are duly impressed with your expertise and the successful forecast of a winner or two during the course of a hearing should clinch the matter. You may try this out by giving the Inspector a few choice tips in correspondence, to show that your system is successful. However, this may be a double-edged sword should the forecast prove to be incorrect!

In the proceedings before the Commissioners you will be given every opportunity to present your case and it is your responsibility to ensure that both you and your adviser are properly prepared for the hearing, to enable you to do your case justice. The Commissioners are likely to be influenced by their own personal knowledge of the area, its personalities and the intrinsic merits of your case. If you have maintained a high profile in an area, you must expect the Commissioners to be aware of it and your reputation. You may experience some difficulty in convincing your adviser that your case warrants the sort of attention that I would consider appropriate. However, the Commissioners are a lay body normally predisposed in favour of a taxpayer so, if you use common sense, you should be able to make sure that you do your case justice.

Letters to Produce and Admit Documents
Your adviser is responsible for making the presentation of your case as easy as possible. There is a procedure for the issuing of 'Letters to Produce' and 'Letters to Admit Documents' that tends to be overlooked.

These items concern the technical admission of evidence and may seem complex to a lay person. For instance, if you or your adviser have sent a letter to the Inspector and you want to produce it in evidence, you will not actually hold the letter concerned, only a copy of the letter at best. In order to get the letter put in, in evidence, the Inspector should be served with a notice to produce the letter at the appeal hearing. If he fails to produce it at the hearing, the Commissioners may admit the copy of the letter, however, having been served with the notice to produce the letter, the Inspector will comply. If you have to resort to putting in a copy of the letter, this can only be carried out by the writer of the letter, introducing the document in the course of giving his evidence to the Commissioners. The writer is the only person on your side who can 'speak' to the letter to have it admitted in evidence. The Inspector, in the course of giving his evidence, may introduce letters and other documents addressed to him by you or your adviser, but he may not introduce any item headed 'without prejudice'.

The request to 'admit documents' refers to accepting that the documents may be admitted in evidence without having to be formally 'proved' before the Commissioners. To prove a document, evidence must be given by the person who brought the document into being or who can give first hand evidence concerning the production of the document and its contents.

Presenting Your Case
The rules of evidence must be adhered to before the Commissioners because there is the underlying possibility that any appeal fought before the Commissioners may go to the High Court on an appeal by the dissatisfied party 'on a point of law' (Section 56 TMA1970). A decision that is a question of fact cannot be appealed against. However, a decision on a question of fact that is not supported by the evidence in the case, or that is considered to be contrary to the evidence adduced at the hearing, has been held to be a question of law. It is, therefore, possible to appeal against virtually every decision of the Commissioners at a contentious appeal against hearing either on the grounds that the decision is contrary to the evidence, or that there is no evidence to support the Commissioners' decision. The Courts will look at the Commissioners' decision in the light of the evidence actually before them at the hearing, so you must ensure that you do not damage your case, by default or lack of presentation.

A more convenient way of proceeding is to have an agreed statement of facts to put before the Commissioners. The skeleton or outline of the case can be agreed with the Inspector beforehand and this enables the Commissioners to have a clear and unequivocal statement of the agreed facts before them. In addition, it assists them to understand the relevance of the evidence that is adduced at the hearing.

The greatest mistake you can make is to overlook the obvious and to assume that the Commissioners have knowledge of facts not actually established *at the hearing*. It is very difficult for Commissioners, or anybody else for that matter, to follow the facts of a case that is entirely foreign to them until the commencement of the hearing. Attendance at Magistrates' or Crown Courts will provide you with some idea of the lengths to which barristers go to ensure that the judges or magistrates have grasped fully the points they wish to make. They carefully go over the same ground from different aspects, reinforcing the points that they consider crucial to their case. It is a lesson that members of the bar have learned from hard experience, and you and your adviser ignore it at your peril. Having identified the documents that need to be produced in evidence, the witnesses to be called, and having prepared a brief setting out the legal arguments and facts in the clearest and best possible tactical order, you should then evaluate the merits, the strengths and the weaknesses of your case. At this stage it may help you to try and anticipate the Inspector's approach, perhaps working through possible questions you may face with an informed but dispassionate friend playing devil's advocate to your witness. Consider what evidence and witnesses the Inspector can produce to undermine your case. How devastating might his cross-examination of your witnesses be? How will your witnesses come across to the Commissioners – are they believable?

When you have fully evaluated your position you should take stock before going ahead. You may negotiate with the Inspector who is anxious to settle the appeal by agreement. The Commissioners, however, have the power to settle the appeal on their own terms and you cannot negotiate with them. If you are failing to impress the Inspector with your arguments and evidence, are you likely to have more success with the Commissioners? The Inspector will be influenced by his assessment of the probable outcome of taking the appeal before the Commissioners. Though he may not welcome the additional work that a formal appeal hearing produces, he will not hesitate to prosecute the Revenue case if you appear unwilling to negotiate a reasonable compromise. Even if you are successful before the Commissioners, the Inspector may express dissatisfaction with the Commissioners' decision and require them to state a case for the opinion of the High Court. You have the same avenue open to you if the positions are reversed but do you wish to run the risk of being involved in all the uncertainty and possible expense of a High Court hearing? The ultimate decision is yours but, in general, it is better to negotiate than to litigate.

7 Commissioners' Precedents?

Very little is known about the activities of the Revenue despite the fact that every member of the tax paying public, and all the public and private companies in the UK are affected by them. Of course, there are periodic reports in the media of tax avoidance cases or Revenue criminal prosecutions. However, the amount of information entering the public domain is very limited, and gives no indication either of the full impact of the law as it is being interpreted by the Revenue, or of the extent to which taxpayers have been engaged in disputes with the Revenue. This is due in part to the number of disputes that are settled privately, and in part to Section 182 FA1989 which protects the confidentiality of individual taxpayer's affairs.

Hearings not open to the public, such as Commissioners' appeal hearings, are not reported and no account of those hearings is available to the general public. Criminal cases do not tend to get reported in full because they are concerned with a jury's interpretation of the evidence adduced in the case, and whether or not it sustains beyond reasonable doubt the charges made. The jury's finding then is one of fact, and provided it is based on the evidence, and the trial has been properly conducted, is not normally capable of being amended. Thus, the proceedings do not establish any legal precedent and are of little general use or application. Although full records of the proceedings are maintained by the Court, they are not generally available to the public. Different juries hearing the same evidence could arrive at different conclusions, and this is why the outcome of a trial is always uncertain. The result of any particular trial does not, therefore, have a direct bearing on the outcome of any other case. Therefore, there is little to be learned from the way in which the jury accepted, or rejected, particular aspects of the evidence, or pleas placed before them. It would be a different matter if the same jury was to be used to try other cases.

In the case of appeals against Court decisions, and any appeals to the

High Court against Commissioners' decisions, the deliberations of the appeal body, or bodies, will be fully reported. Full reports of the proceedings are actually published, and available for inspection and review by any member of the public. Indeed the outcome of such proceedings are studied very carefully by solicitors and barristers who may wish to quote any precedent established by the Courts in support of their own arguments in future cases. They may also rely on the dictum of judges when they comment on aspects of the case that may have a general application. Indeed it must be appreciated, that in order to bring some continuity to the outcome of the proceedings in Courts, and to save the same point being litigated time and time again, Courts accept the precedents established by their peers and will not go against them. The only way in which a past precedent can be overturned is by taking the matter to a superior Court. The Court of Appeal for instance can ignore precedents established by the High Court, and the House of Lords can overturn the rulings of the Court of Appeal. In Scotland, a case may go to the Court of Session and then directly to the House of Lords, since there is no Court of Appeal in Scotland.

Appeals and disputes between the Revenue and taxpayers are first heard by the General or Special Commissioners for Income Tax, the majority being before the General Commissioners. The hearings are in private, no member of the public or press being allowed to be present. The taxpayer may say what he likes about the proceedings, subject to the Civil Law, in particular the law of slander or libel, once outside the hearing. The outcome of the Commissioners' hearings are not reported and no official account of the proceedings is published. It is only if the taxpayer or the Inspector expresses dissatisfaction with the findings of the Commissioners on a point of law that the matter comes into the public arena – appeal proceedings in the High Court and beyond being reported in full.

In order to assist the judicial function, 'privilege' protects certain defamatory statements from action at law. This is a matter of public policy. Qualified privilege enables journalists to publish reports of public judicial proceedings provided the reports are fair and accurate. They may, therefore, report the statements of witnesses that might otherwise be actionable. Once a case goes from the Commissioners to the High Court proceedings are within the public domain and may be reported in the press and elsewhere. The statements of witnesses may then become public knowledge and this should be considered if the taxpayer is sensitive about what witnesses have said about him, or if the claims that the Revenue are seeking to establish may be damaging.

Requesting a Stated Case

The stipulation that a case may only be demanded for presentation to the High Court on a point of law is very important. Judicial comment on what constitutes a point of law maintains that if there is evidence to support a finding of fact by the Commissioners, that finding cannot be overturned. If, however, there is no evidence to support the Commissioners' finding of fact, or if it is contrary to the evidence, then a point of law is involved, and dissatisfaction may be expressed with the Commissioners' determination on a point of law, and a case required to be stated for the opinion of the High Court. The position is clearly set out in Section 56 TMA1970; immediately after the determination of an appeal either party may, if dissatisfied with the determination of the Commissioners 'as being erroneous in point of law, may declare his dissatisfaction to the Commissioners who heard the appeal'. It must be emphasised that there must be an *immediate* expression of dissatisfaction with the decision – you cannot go away and think about the matter. After the expression of dissatisfaction, the person who expressed dissatisfaction has a period of 30 days within which to give written notice to the Clerk to the Commissioners requiring the Commissioners to state and sign a case for the opinion of the High Court. Any such request should be accompanied by the statutory fee, currently £25, for the stated case. There is no requirement, however, that having expressed dissatisfaction with the Commissioners' findings, you must proceed to ask for a case to be stated. You can therefore obtain thinking time by expressing dissatisfaction immediately after the Commissioners' determination, and deciding within the following 30 days whether or not you wish to pursue the matter.

Having obtained the stated case you will have a further 30 days in which to transmit it to the High Court. The Clerk will usually issue copies of the draft stated case for comment by each of the parties to the appeal, before the final version is signed by the Commissioners and issued to the person who has paid the statutory fee. It is obviously important to ensure that the stated case does justice to your cause, and this can only be done during the period of consultation before the stated case is signed by the Commissioners. There is no requirement that the Commissioners accept some, or any part of the representations that you make to them.

The taxpayer may only be represented in any proceedings before the Commissioners by a barrister, a solicitor, or a member of an incorporated society of accountants. This ensures that there is some standard and order in the presentation of an appeal before Commissioners, although there is nothing to prevent the taxpayer representing himself (Section 50 TMA1970).

Commissioner's Precedents?

As contentious investigation cases tend to be based on the determination of the size of the additional assessments made on the taxpayer,
the very nature of the rules governing appeals minimises the number of
cases going to the Courts. An assessment, for instance, can only be
reduced if it appears to the majority of the Commissioners that the
taxpayer has been overcharged by the assessment. The evidence that
they consider may be gleaned by examination of the appellant, the
taxpayer, on oath or affirmation, or by other lawful evidence. Alternatively, it is possible for the Commissioners to increase the assessments
if the evidence supports such action. This could arise if the Inspector
made the additional assessments early on in the enquiry, before the full
measure of the alleged extractions had come to light. The Inspector, in
those circumstances, would not normally raise further assessments in
addition to those already made, and under appeal, although the Board
may claim that the Inspector could take that action if so desired.

The Commissioners' decision will be based, therefore, on the lawful
evidence presented to them, and on the testimony of the taxpayer. If the
taxpayer has made a claim to have received money from non-taxable
sources, and the Commissioners accept the evidence produced to them
in support of the claim, the Inspector cannot successfully express
dissatisfaction with the Commissioners' decision because it will be one
of fact. To challenge the Commissioners' decision the Inspector would
have to be able to show either that there was no evidence to support the
taxpayer's claim, or that the Commissioners' decision was contrary to
the evidence. The taxpayer's success before the Commissioners will,
however, never become common knowledge, although some garbled
account may emanate from the taxpayer. The same, of course, applies
to Revenue successes before the Commissioners.

The Revenue Advantage?
In cases going before the Commissioners the Revenue have a definite
advantage since the District Inspector will be personally involved in
each of the cases taken before them and he will have regular contact
with the Commissioners and their Clerk. Also he may be aware of their
predilections and foibles: it is rather like the prosecutor always having
the same jury, or some permutation of the same jurors. The taxpayers
and accountants on the other hand only have fragmented and infrequent
contact with the Commissioners, although it is possible that your
accountant may act for a Commissioner in his professional capacity. It
is more difficult, therefore, for any person not in close contact with the
Commissioners to make a balanced judgement of what the outcome of
any particular claim made before the Commissioners is likely to be, and
people are naturally wary of the unknown. It is against this background

that the Inspector negotiates with the taxpayer on the additional amount appropriate in his particular case. The result involves a certain amount of bluff and counter bluff about going to the Commissioners for a formal determination of the assessments under appeal.

There has been a fair amount of discussion in the media over the years about the jury system, with comments coming from police officers, politicians, and so on. The natural predisposition of juries to bring in 'not guilty' verdicts when capital punishment was involved, for instance, is commonly known. Nevertheless it has been claimed that mistakes have been made, despite the stringent rules of evidence. The human element enters the equation and the very nature of the crime, or the standing of the accused, may have a bearing on the jury's verdict.

Commissioners for the general purpose of the Income Tax are appointed by the Lord Chancellor. Not a lot is known about the way in which they are vetted or selected, but they tend to form an homogeneous group from the same strata of society and having similar characteristics based on their backgrounds. Bodies of Commissioners may, therefore, take on a unique character of their own that can be self-perpetuating, and to some extent predictable. The District Inspector will use his knowledge of the Commissioners to evaluate the likely chance of success in taking any particular appeal before them. If he feels that the Commissioners might be sympathetic to the taxpayer's claims, the Inspector will be more likely to be conciliatory in his negotiations with the taxpayer. On the other hand, if the Commissioners are likely to come down hard on the particular taxpayer involved, for whatever reason, his stance in negotiations may be more firm.

The Clerk to the Commissioners is selected and appointed by the Commissioners although his remuneration is paid by the Board. The Clerk holds his office 'during the pleasure of the Commissioners and act[s] under their direction' Section 3 TMA1970). The relationship of the Clerk to his Commissioners varies from division to division and depends on the personalities of the individuals concerned. The Clerk normally has a legal background so that he is in a position to advise the Commissioners on the interpretation of the law.

If criminal charges are to be laid against a taxpayer, those proceedings will take precedence over any other action before the Commissioners. It is, however, possible to become involved in a criminal offence if false evidence is given to the Commissioners under oath, the person giving false evidence being open to a charge under the Perjury Act. If this situation is likely to arise the Clerk to the Commissioners may, of his own volition, or at the request of the Inspector, draw the witnesses' attention to the provisions of the Perjury Act.

To return to Commissioners' determination in investigation cases, if the taxpayer loses, and assessments are determined in excess of the amounts returned, the taxpayer is unlikely to advertise the fact. If the Revenue lose, they will just be anxious to forget the proceedings. So it is difficult for you to know which party has been more successful in general, in appeals before the Commissioners. On balance, a taxpayer may achieve a more acceptable result by going before the Commissioners if his representation before the Inspector is weak. In my experience, the Commissioners tend to favour the claims of poorly represented tax-payers, and normally play safe by determining figures midway between those put forward by the taxpayer, and those claimed by the Revenue. I must emphasise, however, that the Commissioners are virtually a law unto themselves and the taxpayer cannot rely on this type of favourable treatment. The taxpayer will also have to consider the actual costs of the hearing before the Commissioners, and the stress involved. The Inspectors are usually realistic in their approach to negotiations and will be prepared to offer a deal equivalent to that likely to be available from the Commissioners. However, an experienced negotiator is needed to achieve the best results and he will begin in a stronger position if the taxpayer has not proved conclusively that he is a liar. If what the taxpayer claims is perhaps a little exaggerated and/or suspect, that is quite different from assertions which have been set out to deliberately mislead the Inspector. For this reason, if for no other, your disclosure statement should withstand critical examination. You do not want a whole series of statements, with each successive one disclosing more assets, or additional income. You should attempt to retain whatever vestige of credibility you can, bearing in mind that your returns and accounts may not have been correct. If a systematic way of understating profits was used, then admission has advantages: the system can be demonstrated, and the understatements pinned to the appropriate level. However, this may strike you as too drastic or potentially expensive an exercise to contemplate. If, as is often the case, no system was operated (beyond helping yourself when necessary to the amount that you thought the business could stand without arousing suspicion), then convincing the Inspector or the Commissioners of the actual level of profit of the business will be more difficult. You will probably not even know what it is yourself! In these circumstances, a sound private side review can be most helpful. Your argument is 'You say I have had all this money, well where is it?'. Although the Inspector is not obliged to show what you have done with the profit he is attributing to your business, this is a telling argument that both he and the Commissioners will understand. To support your private side review keep extremely detailed records of all your private expenditure from the date of the Inspector's challenge. This is tedious in the extreme, but if you have to make a point to the

Inspector or to the Commissioners, they will be more influenced by hard evidence – even though it does not relate directly to the period of the enquiry, and you may have been expected to curtail your spending, at least until you know what the bills from your accountant and the Revenue are likely to total.

When to Go to the Commissioners

Although little is known about the outcome of proceedings before Commissioners, you should consider them as a real alternative to negotiations with the Inspector in appropriate cases. If your accountant is inexperienced in such matters, and you can always ask him, or is reluctant to take on the onerous task of preparing a proper defence brief, then perhaps you should look elsewhere for somebody to represent you. You should certainly see the skeleton or outline of a brief before irrevocably committing yourself to a hearing before the Commissioners. If your accountant cannot convince you by his arguments – and let us face it, you will be anxious to be convinced by them – I suggest that you would be wasting your time and money in going before the Commissioners. Do not, however, be unduly worried by the possibility of the Revenue expressing dissatisfaction with the Commissioners' determination. Just make sure that there is evidence introduced at the hearing to enable the Commissioners to find in your favour as a matter of fact, without any legal complications.

Preparation and Groundwork

Taking appeals before the Commissioners is a measure of last resort, after negotiations with the Inspector have effectively broken down. As an alternative to the Commissioners' hearing you may find that the District Inspector would be prepared to be helpful in resolving any impasse that has been reached. Of course, this action may court further danger! I have personally doubled the amount of the additional income figures considered to be appropriate when reviewing a case previously worked by another Inspector. So appealing to the District Inspector can be a double-edged sword, and needs careful consideration.

The usual opening gambit is that the taxpayer's accountant puts forward the most favourable figures that can reasonably be sustained, with the Revenue putting forward figures that give a less generous interpretation of the same established facts. Each party will maintain his basic position in outline, while without prejudice negotiations take place to reach figures which are acceptable and fair to them both, considering all the circumstances. If there is a particular stumbling point over a specific item, it may be possible to agree figures in the round, that lie midway between the opposing contentions. The overall result may then accommodate items that the Inspector feels he could not possibly allow, while enabling the taxpayer to accept proposed final figures that will perhaps be more generous in areas where there is more room for negotiation. Sensible compromise must be the order of the day if progress is to be made in difficult cases.

If you have a witness that you will need to introduce at an appeal hearing, try to make an independent assessment of how *you* would view him as a witness. Do you actually normally believe what he says, or does he come across as shifty and unreliable, regardless of whether he is telling the truth or not? Will his occupation and general standing in society impress the Commissioners? You could have a dry run by arranging an interview between your potential witness and the Inspector to see how he performs. This may weaken the Inspector's resolve to fight your claim, but on the other hand it may backfire. However, it is a risk worth taking if it saves embarrassment before the Commissioners. The witness should understand, in advance of the hearing, that he may be placed on oath and that his attention may be drawn to the provisions of the Perjury Act.

Finally, as a matter of interest, any documents submitted to the Revenue, and retained in the Inspector's file, are covered by Crown privilege. If the Inspector is subpoenaed to attend any court with the object of introducing the documents in a non- Revenue action, the Inspector will attend as required, but will retain his papers in a sealed package and claim Crown privilege. In such circumstances the papers will be protected and the package will remain unopened.

8 Negotiations

The settlement of an investigation case usually centres round identifiable items of unassessed income, identifiable receipts banked or used to purchase assets or to repay debts, and so on, the source of which cannot be explained, and other amounts about which there is uncertainty. Taxpayers often have a sum in their minds on which they are prepared to settle, to cover the tax lost, interest, and penalties. The Inspector views the matter from quite a different perspective. His only concern is to identify the amount of the undeclared income and its spread or allocation over the period of the enquiry. An arithmetical exercise then follows to compute the tax lost, and the interest eligible under Sections 86 and 88 of the TMA1970. Only the penalty element of the settlement figure is really negotiable.

If the investigation shows that a particular pattern has been followed in making extractions from business profits, or a particular source has been understated or omitted, it may be easier to reach a settlement. Circumstantial evidence and looking at the revised accounts figures with the contemplated additions added back should produce a reasonably consistent picture. Difficulties normally arise in relation to particular items that are claimed by the taxpayer to have come from non-taxable sources.

Every taxpayer must bear in mind the effects of both the statute law as enacted in the taxation acts and the case law that has established the interpretation that is to be placed on the statute law. There are volumes of tax cases containing reports of cases that have gone through the Courts and that have established precedents for the application of various sections of the taxation legislation. The references to tax cases will give the names of the parties to the action, such as *Read* v. *Rollinson*, followed by the volume number (56), the initials TC, identifying the fact that the case appears in the tax case volumes, and a further number (41) stating the page at which the case appears in the tax case volume. The example case will, therefore, be quoted as *Read* v. *Rollinson* 56TC41. If the case is of recent origin and has not yet found its way into the bound tax case volumes, it will be published in leaflet form with just a number such as, *Brittain* v. *Gibb* No3060.

Negotiations

The Commissioners and the Courts are bound by the precedents established in the Courts. However, it is possible for a superior court to override the decision of a lower court. For instance, the Court of Appeal would not feel bound by a decision in the High Court, and the House of Lords would not feel bound by a ruling of the Court of Appeal. Every Court is bound by the precedents established by the House of Lords and Courts of the same standing feel bound by the rulings of their fellow judges.

Taxpayers often have very definite views of their own as to what is just and reasonable. In dealing with the Taxation Acts, however, your own interpretation of them has no relevance and you should be guided by your professional adviser. To illustrate the view that the Courts take of the power of the Commissioners and the Inspector in cases where it is established for one particular year that the business accounts are not accurate and there are unexplained credits to a personal bank account, an example is useful. Here are the details of the basic facts and the decision of Vinelott J. in the Chancery Division on 18 July 1986 in the case of *Brittain* v. *Gibb* (HM Inspector of Taxes):

Mr Brittain was a painter and decorator who also undertook carpentry work. He produced accounts for most of the years under appeal. The Inspector was not satisfied with the accuracy of the accounts and, following an investigation, raised additional estimated assessments. This would have come about in the manner already described. When the matter went before the Commissioners, the Inspector produced evidence showing that there were discrepancies between the taxpayer's records and items shown in the accounts for the year ended 31st July 1981. The Inspector drew the Commissioners' attention to credits to Mr Brittain's current account which were not reflected in the 1981 business accounts, and his wife, who had no known income apart from Child Benefit, had saved a considerable sum during the year. The Inspector's figures were disputed by the taxpayer and he claimed that any errors in his accounts were due to his wife's ill health.

The General Commissioners, after hearing all the evidence, determined the estimated assessments. For some years the assessments were increased and in others they were reduced. They found Mr Brittain guilty of wilful default. The taxpayer expressed his dissatisfaction with the Commissioners' decision on a point of law, contending that the Commissioners ought to have considered his accounts not just for one year but for all the years involved, and that there had not been a fair opportunity to present his case at the hearing.

It was held in the Chancery Division, dismissing the appeal:

67

(1) That the Commissioners, having heard all the evidence, were not satisfied with the accuracy of the taxpayer's accounts. At that point therefore, they became entitled to make their own estimate of what they thought was his probable income from his trade for each year under appeal and it was impossible to say that, in so doing, they erred as a matter of law.

(2) It was not open to the Court upon a Case Stated to consider the question of whether the taxpayer was given a fair opportunity to present his case; that is a matter for application for Judicial Review.

Vinelott J. stated:

It is important that the Appellant, who has appeared in person and has presented his case, if I may say so, very modestly and engagingly, should understand the function of the Court in hearing an appeal from the Commissioners. The Court is required under Section 56(6) of the Taxes Management Act to hear the appeal and determine any question of law arising on the Case Stated. It is well settled that the Court may interfere if the facts found are such that no person acting judicially and properly instructed as to the relevant law could have come to the determination reached by the Commissioners: but the Court has no power to substitute its own conclusion for the conclusion of the Commissioners unless satisfied that they made, or must be assumed to have made, a mistake of law.

The Commissioners heard the evidence of the Appellant and his explanation of accounts of the profits of his trade as a self-employed painter and decorator for the relevant years. Their conclusion was quite simply that they were not satisifed with his explanation of criticisms made by the Inspector as to the accuracy of the accounts which he produced. They accordingly increased the additional assessments for the years 1976–77 to 1978–79, they confirmed the additional assessments for the two years 1979–1980 and 1980-81, they slightly reduced the additional assessment for the year 1981–82 and they increased the estimated assessment for the year 1982–83. In every case they made their own estimate of what they thought was the Appellant's probable income from his trade. In doing so, it is I think clear from the figures, that they arrived at a conclusion by making an estimate of what a self-employed painter and decorator would have charged at an hourly rate and would have expected to make at that hourly rate over the number of hours they estimated he would be likely to work. It seems to be quite impossible to say that in making that estimate, or in rejecting the Appellant's evidence and in particular the accounts he produced, they erred as a matter of law; and, as I have said, it is not for me to form any opinion whether, on the evidence, they ought to have accepted his explanation or made some different estimate.

One point made by Mr Brittain is that the Commissioners erred in principle in that they took his accounts for one year and satisfied themselves that those accounts were not accurate and then proceeded to reject his accounts for all other years, when they ought to have examined his accounts and given reasons for rejecting them in respect of each year. That I think rests on a misconception. The Inspector fastened, not exclusively but to a large extent, upon the accounts for one year in order to demonstrate to the Commissioners that what the Inspector submitted was the unreliability of the Appellant's accounts. The Commissioners, having heard all the evidence, were not satisfied with the accuracy of the accounts, and at that point they were entitled to make their own estimate for each year under appeal.

Another point made by the Appellant is that he was unfairly treated at the hearing in that, when his turn came to address the Commissioners, time was running out and he had no opportunity to put forward all the material that he wished to put before them. . . . As Goulding J. pointed out in *Read* v. *Rollinson* 56TV41 at page 48, a complaint that there was some unfairness or improper conduct in the proceedings before the General Commissioners is not a proper subject for an appeal upon a Case Stated: it is a matter for an application for Judicial Review, where the proceedings before the Commissioners can be examined in detail and where the parties can be given an opportunity to adduce evidence as to the way in which the proceedings were conducted, and so on.

There are a number of important points covered in this judgement that have general application. The most important is that having established that there were inaccuracies in the accounts for one year, that discovery entitled the Inspector to impugn the business accounts for other, earlier, years without going back through the actual records of the individual years concerned in detail. He could take an overall view, having established that the accounts for one year were unreliable, and make estimated additional assessments for the earlier years. The case also illustrates that the Commissioners may adopt any reasonable method to estimate the profits of a taxpayer once the taxpayer's records and accounts have been shown to be inaccurate.

You will also note that due regard was paid to the accumulation of capital by the taxpayer and his wife. It was shown that Mr Brittain's wife had saved a considerable sum during the year when her only known income was Child Benefit and whatever her husband gave to her. Neither the Inspector nor the Commissioners had to prove that the monies came from Mr Brittain's business activities as the onus was on the taxpayer to show that his accounts were correct and complete. Therefore, it was his responsibility to account for the monies that had been accumulated and to show that they did not come from unrecorded business receipts. Although the onus of proof that lies on the Appellant may appear to be Draconian, it is necessary in order to make the taxation system function. More often than not the Inspector is not so much concerned with what has been shown in the business records as with what is missing. It is impossible to show that a particular £5 note was taken by a taxpayer as a business sale but was not actually paid into the till and recorded. Therefore, the onus has been placed on the taxpayer to account for any accumulation of wealth that is apparently inconsistent with his recorded income.

The last thing that you want to attract is the Inspector's attention, and perhaps his dissatisfaction with your accounts and returns. The Inspector is not allowed to be capriciously dissatisfied, so he must have bona fide reservations about your accounts and returns that he can explain to you and, if necessary, to the Commissioners. When carrying out an in depth investigation, the Inspector will aim to establish that there are errors in your records and accounts, to undermine their value as evidence of your full trading profits. He will also attempt to show where these undisclosed profits have gone. These two basic planks of the enquiry will be supported if possible by 'business economics exercises'. These will attempt to highlight variations in gross profit rate percentages on sales over the years that cannot be justified by alterations in the trading mix or by other conditions of the trade or area.

For the taxpayer's part, he is not required by the taxation acts to be a good, effective and efficient businessman, and may well be inept and incompetent. His judgement could have been affected by ill health, he could have suffered stock wastage due to pilfering in various degrees over the years, and so on. He may have exceptionally generous relatives who keep both him and his family in food and clothing. He may never have expensive holidays, and may neither smoke, drink, nor gamble. However, such individuals are very likely to be taken up for investigation: they do not conform to an expected norm.

The Inspector's Judgement
In any investigation the Inspector will view the taxpayer's claims with a somewhat jaundiced eye. He will be accustomed to the fervent lies of taxpayers intent upon preserving either the wealth they have accumulated or, more sadly, the last remnants of their capital. Desperation can

motivate anybody to lie very convincingly and the Inspector will be aware of his limitations when trying to distinguish lies from the truth, or from half-truths. He will be thrown back onto making a judgement based on the balance of probabilities, tempered by his personal knowledge of his own Commissioners and the impact that the taxpayer may be able to make on them as a witness. If, during the course of the investigation, the Inspector can establish that the taxpayer has lied or told part-truths on one or more occasions, then he will claim that the taxpayer's veracity as a witness has been destroyed, and that anything that the taxpayer says should be viewed with the gravest suspicion. Therefore, it is of the utmost importance that you should be able to show that your records are impeccable and cannot be faulted. A brief narrative should be maintained where appropriate to justify marked changes in the profitability of the business, if there have been stock losses you should report the steps taken to minimise them, such as staff changes, security tagging, and so on. Also, were the thefts, or thieves caught, reported to the police?

Your records relating to your private expenditure also need to be reasonably detailed. Cheque stub counterfoils and paying in book details should be completed so that you are able to say at a later date what amounts of cash were drawn, and when; what specific expenditure was met by cheque; and the precise sources of the monies credited to your bank account(s). Your private records must stand up to the same close scrutiny as your business records. It is not unknown for a forward thinking taxpayer to keep cash siphoned off from the business in a hoard at home. Since this cash does not appear in any business records, provided it is only used to meet exceptional rather than normal recurring expenditure and it is not used to acquire assets that are documented, nobody – including the taxpayer – will be able to quantify the amounts involved. The disadvantage is that variations of this scheme are known to be used by the business community and thus they are liable to be burgled. Reporting such losses to the police can lead to unwelcome publicity.

The attraction of extracting business monies gross without paying tax on them is diminished if the money has to be frittered away for fear of detection. The temptation to accumulate large sums is apparently almost irresistible and is often followed by such a golden opportunity either on the business or private front that, despite reservations, caution is thrown to the wind and a purchase is made. Once the hidden cash is transformed into a visible asset, suspicions are often aroused and an investigation tends to follow – with disastrous results for the taxpayer. Not everybody is investigated of course, and a number must evade the net but they have placed themselves in continuing jeopardy.

Understanding Capital Statements

To illustrate some of the points made and the difficulties that can arise on a challenge by the Inspector, the following example sets out details of a ficticious taxpayer's total expenditure of £53,290 (Table 8.1) together with an overall summary showing the sources from which the outgoings have been met (Table 8.2). The alternative figures for cash outgoings £14,080/£13,080 and the corresponding adjustment to the profit/remuneration figures £29,100/£30,100 are merely to show the de minimas effect of unrecorded takings of £1,000 in such a case. I have referred to profit or remuneration because for the purposes of the example it does not matter if you are considering a sole proprietor, a partner, or a director. The Capital Account has been simplified by leaving the lease and investment acquisitions in the revenue expenditure schedule.

The Inspector examining such a case may have only very restricted information concerning the proprietor's capital/drawings account or the director's comparable loan/current account (Table 8.4). The accountant's shorthand may well omit the bequest £6,880 introduced as it was and withdrawn again within the year. There may be no summary of the account provided at all in which case the Inspector would merely have details of the opening balance £5,000, the profit or remuneration figure say £30,100, and the balance carried down £1,000. On the face of it you have drawn £5,000 + £30,100 − £1,000 = £34,100. The Inspector will not know about the betting activities, the £10,000 given to the daughter, or the full cost of the new lease, although your income tax return should refer to the acquisition as it is a chargeable asset.

The payment to the daughter will have to be explained. Was it a gift or a loan? If a loan, what were the terms of the loan concerning interest and/or other consideration and repayment? If a gift, a note may be made for possible inheritance tax purposes. Are there other children and are there any other such gifts?

Your income tax return should show the acquisition of the investment if it relates to a chargeable asset. The Inspector will bear in mind the possibility of income arising from the investment and the lease. The balance sheet will show additions to leasehold premises £5,000 as the introduction of £5,000 does refer to the lease purchased through the private bank account. The accountant may or may not enquire if the full cost was £5,000, what legal expenses are involved, and how they have been dealt with in the books and records of the business.

The Inspector may become aware of the full cost of the new lease (£15,000 plus legal expenses) from the file of the vendor, quite independently of your income tax returns and so on. Information from your daughter's file based on the use made of the £10,000 could also find its way into your papers. The Inspector could conclude that drawings

Table 8.1 Total Expenditure From Bank Accounts 1 and 2 and Cash

Total Outgoings (£)		*A/c 1 (£)*	*A/c 2 (£)*	*Cash (£)*
Sundry Cash	5,000			5,000/4,000
Food	800			800
Clothing	1,000			1,000
Household	300	300		
Boat/Club	1,000	500		500
Telephone	200	200		
Electricity	240	160		80
Water	200	200		
Gas	500	300		200
Community Charge	2,000	2,000		
Mortgage	4,000	4,000		
House Insur.	450	450		
Drink	300			300
Holiday	1,200			1,200
Currency	1,000			1,000
Travellers Cheques	800	800		
School Fees	1,800	900	900	
Investments	2,000	2,000		
New Lease	15,000	10,000	5,000	
Sundry Cheques	500	500		
Credit Card	1,000	1,000		
Daughter	10,000		10,000	
Home Improvements	1,500			1,500
Gambling	2,500			2,500
	53,290	23,310	15,900	14,080/13,080

N.B. Discrepant balance obtained directly from Drawings Account (*see* Drawings Account summary)

Table 8.2 Overall Summary

	Outgoings (£)		*Incomings (£)*
Drawings a/c	10,400	Profit/remuneration	29,100/30,100
Cash a/c	13,080/14,080	Introduced	5,000
Bank a/c1	23,310	Introduced	6,880
Bank a/c2	15,900	Betting Wins	2,000
		Capital Decrease	19,710
	62,690/63690		62,690/63,690

Table 8.3 Capital Account

	Opening figures (£)	Closing figures (£)
Business balance	5,000	1,000
Cash Balance	600	100
Bank account 1	-500	190
Bank account 2	16,000	100
	21,100	1,390

Capital Decrease £19,710

Table 8.4 Drawings Account Summary (in £)

Cash 1,200/2,200		Balance b/d	5,000
800		Profit/Rem.	29,100/30,100
1,700		Introduced	5,000
6,880	10,580/11,580	Bequest	6,880
Bank Transfers	24,000		
NIC	400		
Tax	10,000		
Balance c/d	1,000		
	45,980/46,980		45,980/46,980

Table 8.5 Cash Account

Weekly Expenditure	2,000/3,000	Cash b/d	600
Home Improvements	1,500	Drawings	3,700/4,700
Betting losses	2,500	Bequest	6,880
House Bills	880	Bet. Wins	2,000
Travel	1,200		
Currency	1,000		
Gas	200		
Additional cash	3,800		
Cash Balance c/d	100		
	13,180/14,180		13,180/14,180

Table 8.6 Bank Account 1

Bal. b/d	500 (overdrawn)	Drawings	24,000
Misc. Db.	23,310		
Cr. Bal. c/d	190		
	24,000		24,000

Table 8.7 Bank Account 2

Misc Db.	15,900	Balance b/d	16,000
Balance c/d	100		
	16,000		16,000

Negotiations

Table 8.8 Cash Flow Account

Month	Opening Cash	Cash Drawn	Outgoings		Closing Cash
January	£600	£470	£725	Sundry Cash	(£155)
			£500	Boat/club	
February	(£155)	£470	£725	Sundry Cash	(£1,410)
			£1,000	Clothing	
March	(£1,410)	£470	£725	Sundry Cash	(£1,865)
			£200	Gas	
April	(£1,865)	£470	£725	Sundry Cash	(£3,620)
			£1,500	Home Improvements	
May	(£3,620)	£6,880	£2,200	Holiday	£1,060
June	£1060	£nil	£2,500	Gambling loss	(£1,440)
July	(£1,440)	£470	£Nil		£1,030
		£2,000			
		Gambling Win			
August	£1,030	£470	£80	Sundry Cash	£1,420
September	£1,420	£470	£725	Sundry Cash	£1,165
October	£1,165	£470	£725	Sundry Cash	£910
November	£910	£470	£725	Sundry Cash	£655
December	£655	£470	£725	Sundry Cash	£100
			£300	Drinks	
Opening Cash	£600	£13,580	£14,080	Closing Cash	£100

of some £34,100 are not adequate to finance the purchase of the lease, the investment, and meet the known tax bill and private expenditure. Therefore, the Inspector could proceed to mount a quite ill-founded challenge based on his incomplete knowledge of the facts. It is for this reason that explanatory notes should be forwarded with accounts if a superficial review of the information in the accounts and the tax returns is likely to arouse the interest of the Inspector. Some taxpayers arrange to always draw a regular amount from the business to cover their normal private expenditure and pay the money into their private bank account for use as required. This procedure ensures that their drawings never appear to fall below an acceptable level.

Let us go one stage further and assume that the Inspector is not satisfied with the explanations that he receives and asks for capital, income, and expenditure statements to be prepared. The accountants could produce statements showing the transactions reflected in the bank accounts 1 and 2 but in all probability the cash account would just show cash brought down £600 plus drawings £4,700 and bequest £6,880

75

utilised on private outgoings £12,080 with ending cash in hand £100. The betting winnings of £2,000 and the betting losses of £2,500 would disappear, netted against the general figure for cash outgoings. The cash account may even omit the bequest figure of £6,880 if the introduction was contra'd against the drawings, the cash account showing no bequest, and private expenditure of £5,200 (i.e. £12,080-£6,880), and the accountant worked on this net figure instead of going back either to the Private Ledger, his working papers, or the Cash Book to identify the actual dates and amounts of the drawings made. Therefore, you must assist your accountant and, if necessary, remind him of the bequest, received. The capital, income and expenditure statements must stand close scrutiny, as if they are shown to be incorrect they will damage your standing with the Inspector. The statements should have been seen and approved by you prior to their submission to the Revenue. You will, therefore, have been a party to submitting incorrect statements to the Revenue, and will have undermined your standing in the eyes of the Inspector. If the matter has to go before the Commissioners they will be made aware of your incorrect submission.

Cash Flow Accounts
Looking at the drawings Account Summary (Table 8.4) you will see that £11,580 was drawn in cash. We know that without the betting winnings of £2,000 there would be a cash shortfall of that amount to meet the actual expenditure, but superficially the cash position appears to be satisfactory. However, what if the cash drawings from the business were incorrectly timed and there was in fact a cash flow problem? You will see from the Cash Flow Account (Table 8.8) that, despite the cash position apparently being satisfactory at the year end, there are intermediate months when there is a negative cash position. It is this sort of detailed test that needs to be carried out before the statements are sent to the Revenue. Clearly, the position as set out cannot be correct. Either there are further unrecorded drawings from the business or perhaps private loans have been arranged and the loans repaid on receipt of the bequest that has been cashed through the business.

In this scenario the Inspector will aim to verify the source of the bequest, with confirmation from the solicitor concerned. Any alleged private loans must also be verified, and the Inspector would clearly be intrigued by the existence of bank account 2, the source of its opening balance of £16,000 and the period for which it has been held. It is this sort of factor that may allow the Inspector to break back into earlier years, claiming that he has made a discovery: that a substantial bank account balance existed of which he was unaware when agreeing the accounts. However, the relevance of the bank balance to the business profits could not be established by the Inspector unless he could show that your business accounts and/or income tax returns are incorrect or incomplete, or he can justify the making of additional assessments for the years in which the bank balance was built up.

On the face of it the bequest, presumably received in the form of a cheque, has been cashed through the business bank account. The money was subsequently taken out as drawings. The Inspector may suspect that the cheque may be a business receipt and that it has been passed through the business bank account, either because of the way in which the cheque has been made out, or so that the returned cheque would not suggest that the money had been credited to a private bank account. The cheque may equally well have been paid into the business bank account to meet temporary cash flow problems in the business. Perhaps a large trade debtor has not settled his account as anticipated. You must look at all such transactions through the eyes of the Inspector who is suspicious of everything, to enable you to anticipate his likely follow up questions. A complete explanation of any items which could be misinterpreted should help to assuage any doubts the Inspector may have. It is better to blunt his curiosity at the outset than to have him feel that he is onto something and to become committed to the enquiry. An enquiry may generate a momentum of its own, and the more the Inspector puts into the case, the more difficult it will be for him to give it up.

The Change in the Onus of Proof
Once the Inspector can demonstrate that you have been guilty of neglect and the debate has moved on from whether or not tax has been lost to how much has been lost, over what period, you are really in a quite different position. There is no intermediate situation: either an offence has been committed or it has not. Points can be made in mitigation, explaining how the offence came about, but once you have crossed the line there is no going back. The onus is on the Inspector to establish that something is wrong. He may then put in estimated assessments to recover any tax that may have been lost, and it is up to you to show by lawful evidence that the assessments are excessive. The Inspector may introduce evidence to justify his figures, and in the absence of lawful evidence that the assessments are excessive they must stand as made. However, the Commissioners may increase the assessments if they consider that the evidence justifies such adjustments. In this situation, where only the taxpayer's explanation is available to support his claims, his credibility as a witness is paramount. If he can be shown to have lied, or to have attempted to mislead the Inspector in the past, any subsequent unsupported claims are likely to be heavily discounted.

As the Inspector has no first hand knowledge of what has been going on, he will be seeking circumstantial evidence of the true profitability of the business. Actual profits are reflected in what the taxpayer has accumulated and spent over the period of trading. Looking at the Cash Flow Account the Inspector may well conclude from the regular drawings of £470 per month that the minimum private expenditure is running at that level, i.e. 12 x £470 = £5,640. The withdrawal of the £6,880 in May could be taken as exceptional holiday expenditure perhaps, or part purchase of a property or asset outside the UK, or even the existence of an overseas bank account in the holiday destination. The full holiday cost details should have been sought at the opening interview and the traveller's cheque item in the bank account would have betrayed the existence of the holiday. The Inspector's supposition is that the taxpayer has spent £5,640 + £6,880 = £12,520 – before getting down to the other specific items which may be established. There is, therefore, an apparent cash shortfall to be accounted for by the taxpayer.

If the taxpayer had told the Inspector at the opening interview that he was spending approximately £725 per month on cash outgoings, or if, for a month or two, the drawings figures were in the region of £725 per month, the Inspector would be even more excited, immediately grossing the figure up to £725 x 12 = £8,700 p.a. This figure, plus the bequest of £6,880, would indicate that he had a very promising case on his hands.

The answer is to make sure that your capital, income and expenditure statements are complete and comprehensive: treat your personal accounts as you should your business accounts. They must be capable of withstanding minute examination and the narrative should steer the Inspector in the desired direction. Make it easy for him to agree with your figures and difficult for him to dispute them. The last thing you want to have to do is to provide amended statements because of the valid objections of the Inspector to capital income and expenditure statements that cannot withstand close scrutiny. Your efforts should be directed to being cost-effective: they should support your implicit or actual disclosure of irregularities, and be the *final* word. Do the job once, and do it *properly*.

You must be pragmatic in accepting the burden of proof that falls on you to establish the amount of any understatements. You may be able to engage in some horse-trading with the Inspector concerning the 'greyer' areas, but do not expect the trade to be all one-sided: your adviser should be able to gauge the time to accept a proposal. Also remember that if the matter goes to the Commissioners, they may estimate your profits on any basis that *they* consider appropriate from the evidence before them at the hearing.

Table 8.9 UK Retail Prices Index

Average Index Figs. Calendar Year		*Base Year* 1980	*Base Year* 1974	*Base Year* 1985
Known Expenditure £ (A)		10,000*	5,000*	20,000*
RPI £ (B)		263.7	108.5	373.2
Base Index Fig.£ (C)		37.921	46.082	53.590
1974	108.5	£4,114	£5,000*	£5,814
1975	134.8			
1976	157.1			
1977	182.0	£6,901	£8,386	£9,753
1978	197.1			
1979	223.5			
1980	263.7	£10,000*	£12,151	£14,131
1981	295.0			
1982	320.4	£12,149	£14,764	£17,170
1983	335.1			
1984	351.7			
1985	373.2	£14,152	£17,197	£20,000*
	2942.1 (D)	£111,567	£135,577	£157,667

Overall Totals

	Base Year 1980	*Base Year* 1974	*Base Year* 1985
	(2942.1x 37.921)	(2942.1x 46.082)	(2942.1x 53.590)

(*base year figure).

Note: To calculate the estimated expenditure for any year based on the known expenditure (A) for a given year. Divide known expenditure (A) by the RPI(B) to give a Base Index Figure (C). Multiply this Base Index Figure (C) by the RPI of any chosen year to give the equivalent estimated expenditure for that year.

To calculate the total estimated expenditure for the period multiply the total RPI (D) for the period by the Base Index Figure (C) for the base year chosen.

Applying the Retail Price Index

The Inspector will be interested to see how your level of private expenditure increases from year to year. In cases where evidence of actual expenditure is sparse, figures may be estimated, based on the movements in the Retail Price Index: though an imperfect instrument, it will be readily adopted by the Inspector when he has to produce his own alternative expenditure statements. He will tend to take the year of highest admitted or computed expenditure and use it as a yardstick for each of the other years in question.

A schedule of average UK retail price index figures for the years 1974 to 1985 is set out in Table 8.9. The schedule indicates the interdependence of figures from one year to another. The Inspector will tend to select the year where the highest pound/index figure is produced, and use that figure to establish levels of expenditure for the other years. The year concerned may be based on a relatively short period for which there are high recorded drawings/expenditure, the figures being grossed up to arrive at an annual rate. The scope for distortion of the actual level of expenditure over the years is, therefore, quite large. You can only argue that the 'base' figure should be reduced if you can prove exceptional non-recurring expenditure in the period selected as the 'base' period.

If there is a virtual absence of private expenditure details and there is a year that for one reason or another gives rise to a large balance on the Cash Account that can only be attributed to expenditure, you are likely to have that evidence used against you in a forceful way, lifting your profit figures over the years to possibly unacceptable levels. It is on these occasions that your adviser needs to be at his most persuasive to demonstrate that the business was not capable of producing such profits. Better still are contemporary records of your actual expenditure, with an explanation for the exceptional expenditure involved.

You can see from the examples given in Table 8.9 that expenditure of £5,814 in 1974, £9,753 in 1977, or £14,131 in 1980 and so on would be expanded to produce overall expenditure levels in the region of £157,667 for the period 1974 to 1985. You would have to have a very good story to get the Inspector to accept that you were only spending, say, £10,000 in 1980 if at some particular time you were spending at the rate equivalent to the 1980 rate of £14,131. It is appreciated that the computational results are somewhat arbitrary and possibly unfair to some taxpayers. It is far better that you never place yourself in such jeopardy and have both business and private records that will withstand the closest scrutiny.

The brinkmanship ploy is sometimes adopted to try to test the Inspector's resolve when negotiating figures of omitted income. This can backfire if, as a result of you digging your heels in, the Inspector retaliates by going even deeper into your business and private records to support the claims that he is making. Do not produce statements that may suggest absurd results and negotiate quickly and sensibly across a table: this course of action is far more productive than entering into a sterile duel of words. If you are going to suffer from a paucity of evidence concerning your level of private expenditure, ensure that you keep precise and detailed records of your private expenditure as soon as your records are challenged. You should also tidy up any loose ends in the business records.

If the Inspector can establish that your accounts are inaccurate, the next question is for how long have they been inaccurate? Have they always been inaccurate since the commencement of the business or is there some particular event that you can identify as the commencement of your peccadillos? If you cannot say why or when the irregularities began, and give some reasonable account of the events concerned, supported by circumstantial evidence of available income being sufficient to meet your outgoings prior to the 'happening', then you are in real trouble. You should also be able to show that you took immediate action to cease practicing the procedures that have given rise to the understatements. In other words you need to establish dates of commencement and cessation of the irregularities so that the Inspector's enquiries are contained within that period.

You should also consider the instructions given to your accountant concerning the preparation of your accounts and the work for which they are responsible. While the Revenue will not allow any taxpayer to hide behind the inadequacies of his accountant, you may seek recompense for any liability incurred due to your accountant's negligence. It may be appropriate and advisable in this case to employ a firm of accountants specialising in Revenue enquiries to carry out the investigation work, and some firms employ former Inspectors who have served in the Revenue Enquiry Branch and Special Office, who are ideally qualified to protect your interests. They will probably make a better job of the investigation report and will be available to give evidence of your former accountant's shortcomings, should you wish to establish a claim against the accountants who prepared your accounts.

You should always bear in mind that the allocation of extractions over the years can have a marked effect on the final offer required to settle the Revenue's claims. The rate of tax at which you will be liable, and the build up of interest under Section 88 TMA1970 in respect of the earlier years are points to be noted. When figures of assessable income are revised all the taxation consequences of that revision flow from the new figures. Loss relief claims, for instance, may have to be amended to take into account the higher levels of profit available to utilise losses brought forward. If, when the original loss figures are adjusted for the extractions made, either a reduced loss, or a profit emerges, the loss relief already allowed will have to be revised. Class 4 National Insurance contributions are levied with the income tax for trades, professions or vocations, chargeable under Case I or II of Schedule D. Therefore, amendment of the figures of assessable profit may affect the amount of the Class 4 contributions due. Any additional amounts of Class 4 National Insurance owing due to a taxpayer's fault carry interest under Section 88 TMA1970 (Social Security Act 1975 Sch. 2 para. 7). If the Class 4 figure has to be increased because of amendments to the figures of assessable profit, the additional National Insurance will be included in the settlement, together with any additional Section 88 interest. No penalties are chargeable in respect of the underpaid Class 4 National Insurance contributions. The VAT returns may have to be revised if the nature of the extractions effect the VAT liability of the business. However, this is a separate matter and should be taken up with the Customs and Excise department direct, though the revised figures for taxation purposes should include the appropriate VAT adjustments.

9   DIY Statements

It may be tedious and time consuming to prepare your own Capital, Income and Expenditure Statements but the difficulties involved are not insurmountable. People tend to be put off by figure work, but if you can write up simple business records and operate a pocket calculator, there is no reason why you should not prepare sound Capital, Income and Expenditure Statements.

Most of us are familiar with standard business record books such as *Simplex* which take you stage by stage through keeping weekly balanced cash accounts to the preparation of Trading, and Profit and Loss Accounts, and Balance Sheet merely by transferring the various prepared totals to the appropriate places in the skeleton pre-printed pages at the back of the book. The Capital, Income, and Expenditure Statements follow precisely the same principles and format, but are if anything more straightforward, not needing adjustments for stock, work in progress, or accrued expenses and so on. The secret is to keep the preparation of the statements as simple as possible, and to ensure that the summaries that you prepare for the Cash and Bank Accounts actually balance. Arithmetical mistakes can make a nonsense of your work and, with the availability of pocket calculators, are really quite inexcusable.

The similarity between the standard business records of the *Simplex* type and the records required for the private side Capital, Income and Expenditure Statements arises because in the private side statements you are treated as though you are a business in your own right. The Trading and Profit and Loss Accounts, instead of reflecting business transactions, shows private incomings such as drawings, dividends, interest, gifts, gambling winnings, student letting, and other non business rental income etc. The outgoings, instead of business expenses, refer to all your private outgoings on rent, community charge, mortgage, light, heat, food, clothing, holiday and so on. The resultant profit or loss derived from the surplus of incomings over outgoings, or the surplus of outgoings over incomings, will reflect the net increase, or decrease, in wealth over the year. As with a business account, however, not every transaction passes through the Trading or Profit and Loss Account *in toto*. Some transactions will be of a capital nature, such as the sale and replacement of a business car. In your business accounts the car sold will be taken out of the Balance Sheet and the replacement vehicle shown as an acquisition: only the loss or profit on the disposal of the old vehicle will be reflected in the Profit and Loss Account. The same rules apply to the private side Capital, Income and Expenditure Statements. The sale of your house, private vehicle or boat will be reflected in the Balance Sheet or Capital Account, and any replacement item will be shown in its place. The Profit and Loss Account, and the Income and Expenditure statements in the private side review will show the profit or loss, i.e. surplus of deficiency, made on the disposals by comparing the net amount realised on the disposal, with the figure at which it was shown in the previous year's Capital Statement.

The Starting Point
Where should you start on the preparation of your first set of Capital, Income and Expenditure Statements? I suggest that you begin by going through your business records and extracting the details shown for sums introduced by you into the business and the drawings made. The figures should be contained in the summary at the end of your business Cash Book, but you should check these figures against those actually shown in your business accounts as submitted to the Revenue as accountants sometimes make adjustments to the figures in the prime business records when preparing the business accounts. Adjustments can arise from the incorrect posting of items that are private to a business expense heading, or vice versa. There may also be an unaccounted for balance on the Cash Account that may have been cleared by the accountant as capital introduced or drawings, depending on whether the balance was a surplus of computed cash over the figure shown in the business records or a cash deficiency. For whatever reason, the figures recorded in the business records may differ from those in the accounts and you should adopt the figures used in the accounts when preparing your Capital, Income and Expenditure Statements. If there is any differences or adjustments you do not understand, ask your accountant to provide you with a full summary of the Capital and Drawings Accounts from his working papers.

A word of warning: too many businesses rely on computed figures of cash in hand, rather than on a physical count of the money involved. There is *no* substitute for an actual count of the money. It is the most effective cross-check of the accuracy of the arithmetic flowing from the figures shown in the business records. It also prevents you from happily recording a minus figure for cash in hand, an error so often found in less sophisticated business records.

Using the same example figures as are shown in Chapter 8 (*see* Tables 8.1–8.8) let us assume the Drawings Account summary shows:

DIY Statements

	£		£
Cash drawn	10,580	1988 Cr. Capital a/c bal. b/d	5,000
Bank tfers	24,000	Introduced	11,880
NIC	400	Profit/Remuneration	29,100
Tax	10,000		
1989 Cr. bal. c/d.	1,000		
	45,980		45,980

You can now proceed in one of two alternative ways: you can decide to show the Capital Account balances on your Capital Statements also including the profit/remuneration figure in the Income Statement, or you can simplify matters by only showing the net amount drawn in your Income Statements, and dealing with the various debits to the Drawings Account in your Cash Account and Expenditure Statements. The outcome will be correct whichever basis you adopt as can be illustrated by the example set out later in this chapter.

The next step is to annotate the Drawings Account summary, identifying the source of the monies introduced, the accounts to which the bank transfers have been made, and the uses made of cash drawn. Again referring to the example in Chapter 8, Table 8.4 the notes may look like the following:

	£				£
Cash drawn	10,580	Cash a/c 1988	Capital bal.b/d		5,000
Bank tfers	24,000	Bank a/c1	Introd. cash a/c	5,000	
NIC	400	Expend. a/c	Bequest	6,880	11,880
Tax	10,000	Expend. a/c	Profit/Rem. Income a/c		29,100
1989 Cr. Cap. bal c/d	1,000	1989 Cap. a/c.			
	45,980				45,980

The initial entries for the Cash Account will then be:

	£		£
		1988 Cash in hand b/d	600
Introd. cap. a/c	£11,880	Drawings	10,580
1989 Cash in hand c/d	100		

The draft Cash Account can then be put to one side to await further entries as you proceed to draw up summaries of each bank account, investment account, and so on.

The bank account summaries will again show the same figures as those used in the example in Chapter 8 Table 8.6.

Bank Account 1

	£			£	
1988 o/d bal. b/d	500	Drawings		24,000	Bk. a/c tfers
Misc. debits	23,310				
1989 Cr. bal c/d	190				
	24,000			24,000	

You will have identified the source of the regular transfers from the business bank account, and from the cheque book stubs you can broadly summarise the miscellaneous cheques. It is advisable to note the nature of the outgoing against the relevant entry in the bank statements and to draw a line across the bank statements at the terminal date adopted for the business accounts and Capital, Income and Expenditure Statements. If any transfer to or from the private bank accounts included in the business records has not been dealt with in the bank statements to the terminal date, it will be necessary either to amend the bank statement total, or to note to make an adjustment to debtors or creditors in the private Capital Statements, to take the transaction into account.

We know that the miscellaneous debits of £23,310 consist of the following items:

	£	
Household Expenditure	300	General living expenses
Boat/Club	500	Hobby
Telephone	200	
Electricity	160	Recurring household expenditure.
Water rate	200	Note to ensure full amount
Gas	300	accounted for and no regular
Community charge	2,000	payment for any quarter
Mortgage payments	4,000	is missing.
House insurance	450	
Traveller's cheques	800	Holiday – any refund?
School fees	900	Each term's fees shown?
Investments	2,000	Cap.a/c – any dividends?
Lease	10,000	How dealt with in accounts?
Sundry cheques	500	General living expenses
Credit card	1,000	Make up of expenditure?
	23,310	

DIY Statements

Make notes against each item indicating if it is to be posted to the Expenditure Account or to the Capital Account, and whether or not there are further payments to be accounted for in either the Bank or the Cash Accounts.

Bank Account 2

	£		£
Misc. debits	15,900	1988 Bal. b/d	16,000
1989 bal. c/d	100		
	16,000		16,000

Clearly the Inspector will be curious about the source of the £16,000 and why it has been held in an account that is not producing any interest. You will need to explain the matter as clearly and concisely as possible, in such a way as to pre-empt supplementary questions. Your stance will depend on how sure you feel about yourself, and the accuracy of your business accounts and income tax returns. You can only afford to politely tell the Inspector to mind his own business if the Inspector cannot demonstrate that your account and/or income tax returns are either incomplete, or incorrect. You should be able to show that you have been reasonably forthcoming in the explanation volunteered about the £16,000 and that in your view, the Inspector ought to be satisfied with that explanation.

We know from Table 8.1 in Chapter 8 that the miscellaneous cheques consist of the following items:

	£	
School fees	900	Cross refer to items in bank a/c1 (i.e. total £1,800) – were any further amounts paid? If a boarder, the level of private living expenditure will be affected. Any additional fees for sports, uniform, and such like?
New lease	5,000	Is this item dealt with as capital introduced? Why was not the full £15,000 shown on the balance sheet? This is already capitalised in the business balance sheet.
Daughter	10,000	You will need to explain the background and nature of this transaction. Liaise with daughter and discuss.
	15,900	

As there are no other bank, savings, or other accounts, we are now left with the Cash Account to construct. The items to be cleared through the

Cash Account are:

	£		£	
Private cash exp.	4,000	1988 Bal. b/d	600	
Food	800	Cash drawn	3,700	When drawn?
Clothing	1,000	Bequest	6,880	Why cash?
Boat/club	500	Betting wins	2,000	Evidence?
Electricity 1 qtr	80			
Gas (2 qtrs)	200			
Drink/entertainment	300			
Holiday travel	1,200			
Holiday currency	1,000			
Home improvements	1,500			
Gambling losses	2,500			
1989 Bal. c/d	100			
	13,180		13,180	

Presentation of the Figures
It is at this stage that a great deal of thought must be taken to decide how your figures are to be presented. You should clearly comment on the opening cash position, stating what evidence you have that you held £600 in cash at the beginning of the year in 1988.

The bequest should be documented and evidence of the payment of the £6,880 sought from the person from whom the payment was received. If it is the balance of an estate account you have administered, accounts can no doubt be produced to show the amount inherited.

The gambling situation is more delicate. It could be argued that the inclusion of the net loss of £500 (i.e. £2,500 lost, £2,000 won = £500) in the total private expenditure figure, without being separately distinguished, correctly, if not fully, represents your gambling activities.

You should separately identify the electricity and gas bills met from the Cash Account to demonstrate to the Inspector that you have identified the full expenditure involved.

Tactics enter into the presentation of the other figures. You could show:

	£	£
Electricity (1 qtr)		80
Gas (2 qtrs)		200
Other expenditure		
Cash food and clothing	5,800	
Boat/club	500	

DIY Statements

Drink, travel and holiday	2,500	
Home improvements	1,500	
Net gambling loss	500	10,800
1989 Bal c/d		100
		11,180

i.e. £13,180 less gambling wins £2,000

Clearly you will not be able to recall accurately all your cash expenditure, and the figure for other private expenses will in effect be a balancing figure derived from the opening cash in hand, plus identified cash receipts, less closing cash in hand and any specific cash expenditure you have identified.

The overall figure for miscellaneous private cash expenditure of £10,800, plus specific items of £280 (£11,080) could be an embarrassment if, for example, you had only around £6,380 in the previous year. By your presentation of the 1988/9 figures you may actually raise doubts in the Inspector's mind concerning the adequacy of the 1987/88 figures. Let us suppose that you took no holiday in 1987/88 and consequently had not incurred expenses of £1,000 on holiday clothing. Similarly, that year there were no boat expenses, no outlay on home improvements, and so on. Viewed in this light the comparative figures are:

	1987/88 £	1988/89 £
Private expenses	6,380	5,300
Clothing		1,000
Boat/club		500
Entertainment and holiday		2,500
Home improvements		1,500
Electricity		80
Gas		200
	6,380	11,080

If there has been a material change in the level and pattern of expenditure, it is advisable to identify specific non-recurring items that are disturbing the pattern of private expenditure from one year to another. Otherwise the Inspector may suspect that if you required £11,080 to meet your needs in 1989, did you not require a comparable amount in 1988 to maintain your life style? His conclusion could be that the additional amount required to meet the difference between the figures for 1988 and 1989 has been funded from undeclared profits of the business. Therefore,

89

it is better to head off such thoughts by covering the matter in the presentation of your statements, and in the accompanying narrative.

The end products of your efforts are your Capital, Income and Expenditure Statements which will look like Tables 9.1, 9.2 and 9.4.

Table 9.1 Capital Account

	1988 £		1989 £
Business Capital a/c	5,000		1,000
Cash in hand	600		100
Bank a/c 1	(-500)		190
Bank a/c 2	16,000		100
New lease		Bank a/c 1	10,000
Daughter (loan?)		Bank a/c 2	10,000
Home improvements		Cash a/c	1,500
Investments		Bank a/c 1	2,000
Opening Capital	21,100	Closing Capital	24,890
		Less Opening Capital	21,100
		Increase in Capital	3,790

Table 9.2 Income and Expenditure Account 1989

		Income	£
		Profit/Remuneration	29,100
		Bequest	6,880
		(Betting wins netted with loss)	
			35,980
Expenditure	£		
Cash a/c	9,580	(11,080-capitalised 1,500)	
Bank a/c 1	11,310	(23,310-capitalised 12,000)	
Bank a/c 2	900	(15,900-capitalised 15,000)	
Drawn a.c			
Tax	10,000		
NIC	400	Total Expenditure	32,190
		To Net Increase Capital	3,790

The Expenditure Summary is set out in full in Table 9.3.

90

DIY Statements

Table 9.3 Expenditure Summary

	Cash a/c £	Bank a/c 1 £	Bank a/c 2 £	Drawings £	Totals £
Private cash	4,800	800	—	—	5,600
Clothing	1,000	—	—	—	1,000
Boat/club	500	500	—	—	1,000
Electricity	80	160	—	—	240
Gas	200	300	—	—	500
Drink, etc.	300	—	—	—	300
Holiday/travel	1,200	—	—	—	1,200
Currency	1,000	800	—	—	1,800
Gambling *(net loss)*	500	—	—	—	500
Telephone	—	200	—	—	200
Water	—	200	—	—	200
Community charge	—	2,000	—	—	2,000
Mortgage	—	4,000	—	—	4,000
House insur	—	450	—	—	450
School Fees	—	900	900	—	1,800
Credit card	—	1,000	—	—	1,000
Tax	—	—	—	10,000	10,000
NIC	—	—	—	400	400
Totals	9,580	11,310	900	10,400	32,190

Table 9.4 Alternative Presentation of Expenditure Summary

You may now revamp the figures to arrive at the headings and amounts considered most appropriate to present your case in the best possible light, perhaps as follows:

	£
General private expenses	9,400
Gas, light and heat	740
Community charge and water rates	2,200
Mortgage	4,000
Insurance – house, etc.	450
Telephone	200
Exceptional holiday expenses	3,000
School fees	1,800
Tax	10,000
NIC	400
Total	32,190

91

The exact format can be adapted to that most suited to your needs.

The process I have described may seem somewhat daunting, but it is in fact perfectly straightforward. If desired you could purchase a spare Simplex type record book, and merely enter the details of your private transactions from your drawings and bank account records as though you were writing up your business records in the normal way. The resulting Trading, Profit and Loss, and Balance Sheet represent the private side Capital, Income, and Expenditure Statements you are seeking.

The Alternative Presentation

An alternative presentation of the statements, excluding the business Capital Account balances, and the trading Profit/Remuneration figures is:

Capital Account

	1988 £	1989 £
Cash in hand	600	100
Bank a/c1	(-500)	190
Bank a/c2	16,000	100
New lease	—	10,000
Daughter (loan?)	—	10,000
Home improvements	—	1,500
Investments	—	2,000
	16,100	23,890
Less Brought Forward		16,100
Net Capital Increase		7,790

Income and Expenditure

	Income £		
Drawings	44,980	Cash	10,580
		Bank tfers	24,000
		NIC	400
		Tax	10,000
Less introd.	11,880	Bank a/c 2	5,000
		Bequest	6,880

DIY Statements

Net drawings   33,100
Addl. income bequest 6,880
Net total income   39,980

Expenditure £

Cash	9,580		
Bank a/c1	11,310		
Bank a/c2	900		
Drawings a/c tax	10,000		
Drawings a/c NIC	400	Total exp.	32,190
		Net Capital Increase	7,790

The difference between the net capital increase of £7,790, using the above method, and that incorporating the capital balances – £3,790 – is easily reconciled. The closing Capital Account balance of £1,000 shows a diminution of £4,000 from the opening Capital Account balance of £5,000. It is the exclusion of the Capital Account balances that increases the capital wealth increase figure by £4,000 above the original net increase shown. The adjustment for the Capital Account balances is taken into account automatically by taking the net drawings figure of £33,100 and excluding the profit/remuneration figure of £29,100. As the net drawings figure exceeds the profit/remuneration figure by £4,000, there must be a similar increase in the net capital increase figure. The two adjustments of £4,000 to the capital wealth figure and the net income less expenditure figure effectively cancel each other out, so that the net income less expenditure still agrees with the net increase in capital wealth.

Returning to the presentation aspect of the statements, if the amount available to meet private expenditure is sub-standard, it has been known for a number of items to be lumped together, to make the statements look more acceptable. In the example quoted, for instance, failure to specifically identify and capitalise the amount spent on home improvements (£1,500), and some, or all, of the holiday expenditure (£3,000) could made a substantial difference to the amount available to meet private expenditure, i.e.

£9,400 + 1,500 + 3,000 = 13,900.

The overall statements will still balance:

Capital Account

	1988 £			1989 £
	16,100			23,890
		Less home improvements		1,500
		Less b/f		16,100
		Net Capital Increase		6,290

Income (As before)	39,980	
Expenditure		
(As before) 32,190		
Plus impr. 1,500		
Net Capital Increase	6,290	

Presentation can make the world of difference to how the figures will look to the Inspector, without upsetting the balance of the statements.

If you can draw up statements for one year, there is no reason why you should not do the job for as many additional years as are necessary. As an incentive you should ask your accountant to give you a quote for doing the work for you. I am sure the reply will provide sufficient motivation for you to do at least the preparatory work, such as producing bank account summaries and so on, even if you do not undertake all the work yourself.

When to Start

You will obviously not wish to attempt to draw up Capital, Income, and Expenditure Statements just for the fun of it, but you should realise that, when facing a serious challenge to your accounts and/or income tax returns by the Inspector, the assistance provided by such statements could be invaluable. They will crystallise the established outline of your affairs in your own mind, and highlight the areas that could be of mutual concern to you and the Inspector. The Inspector should be asked to specify both the particular area that is causing disquiet and the period he has under review. Statements should be prepared for the full period involved plus one earlier year, to provide a safety margin. It is also a good idea to ask the Inspector to provide you with copies of your relevant income tax returns if you do not already have them.

Having obtained the Inspector's written comments concerning the nature and area of concern, you can explore your overall position and either satisfy yourself that you are in the clear, or to take on board the fact that the Inspector has a valid point. Anticipate any possible request for Capital, Income and Expenditure Statements and have them available, for your own benefit, when dealing with any points the Inspector raises in correspondence. In this way you will learn in advance what has to be accounted for, and when it arose. You may also have a fairly clear picture of the full amount and period involved, as distinct from that which emerges from the Capital, Income, and Expenditure Statements, based on the information and documents that you have produced.

If you are far sighted, you may adopt a *modus operandi* that will ensure that no matter how dubious the circumstantial evidence is, that there is no positive evidence available to the Inspector to impugn your accounts or income tax returns. It is also possible to keep your affairs straightforward by ensuring that the sources of all monies credited to your bank accounts etc. are fully recorded in paying in books, and that you systematically draw the amounts of cash necessary to meet an acceptable level of private expenditure.

Cash – the Flexible Friend

In the case of miscellaneous cheques and the balance on the Cash Account adopted as the overall level of private expenditure for any period, it is clearly desirable to identify exceptional items of expenditure if the overall level is higher than that of adjacent years. On the other hand, if the amounts available are on the low side, identifying specific items of exceptional expenditure is unproductive from the taxpayer's point of view. There is more room to manoeuvre if specific bills are not paid direct by cheque. Instead, if cheques are made out for round sum amounts of cash, and bills settled from an ongoing cash pool, there will be less room for dispute with the Inspector. Cash, in these circumstances, *is* your flexible friend.

There are, of course, limits to the extent to which cash can be flexible. It is not available to meet expenditure before it has been drawn, and the drawing of fresh amounts of cash could be interpreted as indicating that the bulk of any existing cash accumulation had been, or was about to be, exhausted. The claim to have a large accumulation of cash when you are at the same time running a bank overdraft, is not likely to be accepted without details of the reason for such apparently unusual behaviour. One reason may be that your bank manager has placed too much pressure on you regarding the way in which you operate your bank account and dictates the maximum amount that can be drawn from the account. The Inspector would, however, wish to hear the tale from your own lips.

You must ensure that the overall results shown by your statements are capable of withstanding critical examination by the Inspector. If there are discrepancies for which no explanation is forthcoming, it is better than any incomings from unidentified sources, or dubious sources such as betting wins or unsubstantiated gifts, are quantified and incorporated in your statements. The Inspector should be presented with a complete set of defensible statements to which you can hold, otherwise you put yourself on the slippery slope of having to change your stance, forced by inconsistencies in your statements to accept that substantial amendments should be made to them. By all means be prepared to negotiate with the Inspector and, if necessary, to reluctantly do a deal whereby, under a compromise, without prejudice agreement, you may be prepared to accept additional assessments treating some part of the dubious items as unassessed income. There is nothing to prevent you being generous and realistic concerning any lack of evidence that you may have concerning the matters in dispute.

As the taxpayer involved in running the business you are in an excellent, authoritative position to explain any discrepancies in relation to your statements and business accounts. The Inspector can only draw *inferences* from the documentary evidence that you have caused, one way or another, to have been brought into existence, and from your personal testimony. If the Inspector cannot fault the moderate and accurate statements produced, any criticism is blunted, and he can only point to items, if any, 'voluntarily' disclosed in your statements. Damage limitation is an important exercise and will persuade the Inspector that he should settle rather than prolong a possibly unproductive investigation.

Take a broad overall view of the Capital, Income, and Expenditure Statements before approving their submission to the Revenue to see if anything has been overlooked. Always remember that *whoever* prepared the statements, *you* must take full responsibility for their content. You cannot hide behind any shortcomings of your accountant, but you cannot be expected to be personally endowed with the accountant's expertise.

10 Company Investigations

In the case of a company investigation the individual directors come under enquiry in addition to the company itself: similarly irregularities in the tax returns of a director may bring about an investigation of his company. The same criterion applies to partners and partnerships.

The company, though a separate legal entity, can only act through its officers. The Revenue consider that they have the right to raise alternative assessments on the company under the Corporation Tax provisions in respect of alleged understated profits of the company, and on the directors under Schedule E in respect of their share of those undeclared profits as additional emoluments of their office as directors of the company. If the extractions are such that, when the directors' loan or current accounts are re-written to take the extractions into account, the accounts are overdrawn, the overdrawn balances are assessed under the provisions of Section 419 ICTA1988 as loans or advances to the directors. Section 419 states;

(1) Subject to the following provisions of this section, where a close company, otherwise than in the ordinary course of a business carried on by it which includes the lending of money, makes any loan or advances any money to an individual who is a participator in the company or an associate of a participator, there shall be assessed on and recoverable from the company, as if it were an amount of corporation tax chargeable on the company for the accounting period in which the loan or advance is made, an amount equal to such proportion of the loan or advance as corresponds to the rate of advance corporation tax in force for the financial year in which the loan or advance is made.

(2) For the purposes of this section the cases in which a close company is to be regarded as making a loan to any person include a case where:

(a) that person incurs a debt to the close company, or
(b) a debt due from that person to a third party is assigned to the close company,

97

and then the close company shall be regarded as making a loan of an amount equal to the debt.

Section 420(1) provides that Section 419(2) (a) above

shall not apply to a debt incurred for the supply by the close company of goods or services in the ordinary course of its trade or business unless the credit given exceeds six months or is longer than that normally given to the company's customers.'

There are certain exempt loans referred to in Section 420(2) as follows:

(2) Section 419(1) of this section shall not apply to a loan made to a director or employee of a close company, or of an associated company of the close company if:
(a) neither the amount of the loan, nor that amount when taken together with any outstanding loans which–
(i) were made by the close company or any of its associated companies to the borrower, or to the wife or husband of the borrower, and
(ii) if made before 31st March 1971, were made for the purpose of purchasing a dwelling which was or was to be the borrower's only or main residence;
exceeds £15,000 and the outstanding loans falling within sub-paragraph (ii) above do not together exceed £10,000; and
(b) the borrower works full-time for the close company, or any of its associated companies, and
(c) the borrower does not have a material interest in the close company or in any associated company of the close company but if the borrower acquires such a material interest at a time when the whole or part of any such loan made after 30th March 1971 remains outstanding the close company shall be regarded as making to him at that time a loan of an amount equal to the sum outstanding.

Section 419(3) states:

Tax shall be assessable by virtue of this section whether or not the whole or any part of the loan or advance in question has been repaid at the time of the assessment and tax assessed by virtue of this section shall, subject to any appeal against the assessment, be due within fourteen days after the issue of the notice of assessment.

The Section 419 tax is repayable when the loans or advances are refunded to the company under the provisions of Section 419(4), but any interest arising on the unpaid tax by virtue of Sections 88 or 86 is not repayable and neither is any penalty exigible under the provisions of the taxation acts. Section 419(4) states:

> Where a close company makes a loan or advance which gives rise to a charge to tax on the company under subsection (1) above and the loan or advance or any part of it is repaid to the company, relief shall be given from that tax, or a proportionate part of it, by discharge or repayment
>
> Relief under this subsection shall be given on a claim, which must be made within six years from the end of the financial year in which the repayment is made.

The provisions of Section 419 are broadly to discourage directors from taking money out of a company tax-free, as a loan, rather than as a taxed dividend or remuneration. It puts the company in basically the same position, subject to relief under Section 419(4) on repayment of the loan, as a company paying a dividend equal to the amount of the loan. It should not be overlooked that under the provisions of Section 160 ICTA1988 the loan or advance would normally be treated as a benefit in the hands of the director. This additional liability is not, however, charged under Sch.E when the Section 419 tax carries interest under Section 88 and penalties.

In considering possible Section 419 liability, the various balances of the directors are not lumped together. It is possible, therefore for Section 419 liability to arise on one or more directors' current and or loan account balances as they become overdrawn, while other directors remain in credit. The credit balances are not available for setting off against the overdrawn balances. An example of the type of computation involved is set out in Table 10.1.

Re-writing the Current/Loan Accounts

At the conclusion of the enquiry when the current/loan accounts are rewritten, the director's actual position *vis à vis* the company is amended and, if overdrawn, the company will be able to pursue the debts due from the director (or perhaps from his estate). Furthermore, the benefit provisions of Section 160 ICTA1988 will establish liability under Sch.E in respect of any residual beneficial loans or advances outstanding in the post-enquiry years.

Table 10.1 shows the director's original credit balances on his loan account, together with the amount of the extractions made each year. The revised director's loan account balances flowing from the cumulative

Table 10.1 Section 419 Computations

Chargeable Accounting Periods Y/E 31 March	Dir.Bal. Loan a/c £	Extractions £	Cumulative Extractions £	Revised Loan Account Bal. £	ACT Rate £
1979	Cr 1,000	1,500	1,500	(500)	33/67
1980	5,000	1,000	2,500	2,500	3/7
1981	7,500	2,000	4,500	3,000	3/7
1982	3,000	3,000	7,500	(4,500)	3/7
1983	2,000	2,000	9,500	(7,500)	3/7
1984	8,000	5,000	14,500	(6,500)	3/7
1985	18,000	10,000	24,500	(6,500)	3/7
1986	30,000	500	25,000	5,000	3/7
1987	17,000	1,000	26,000	(9,000)	29/71
1988	10,000	1,000	27,000	(17,000)	27/73
1989	5,000	3,000	30,000	(25,000)	1/3
1990	35,000	nil	30,000	5,000	1/3
		30,000			

	S.419 Liability (£)	S. 419(4) Repayment (£)
1979	246.26	
1980		246.26 (5,00 X 33/67)
1981		
1982	1,928.57	
1983	1,285.71	
1984		428.57 (1,000 X 3/7)
1985		
1986		2,785.71 (6,500 X 3/7)
1987	3,676.05	
1988	2,958.90	
1989	2,666.66	
1990		9,301.61(9,000 X 29/71)
		(8,000 X 27/73)
		(8,000 X 1/3)
	12,762.15	12,762.15

Liability to penalties arises on £12,762.15. Interest is exigible under S.88 if assessments made for purposes of recovering tax lost are due to neglect or similar failure.

Credit is due for interest purposes in respect of the S.419(4) relief.

The same principles apply in computing the liability of later accounting periods.

extractions figures are also shown. The Section 419 liability arises on the overdrawn balances at the advance corporation tax rate applicable to the financial year in which the accounting period ends. The Section 419(4) repayment or set off refers back to the earliest Section 419 assessments first and to the rates to which the overdrawn balances have been charged, and only moves on to later periods when the amounts of the earliest assessments have all been repaid or set off. The six year time limit for making claims under Section 419(4) is not applied to investigation cases, where the liability itself may not come to light until more than six years after the end of the year concerned. In addition, it must be noted that the Section 419 liability exists even if at the time of making the assessment the loan has been repaid. This is to close an obvious loophole: to prevent taxpayers avoiding the liability by repaying the loan before an assessment can be made. It should also be noted that if a director makes a loan to his company and shows the loan as a separate and distinct account in the balance sheet and so on in addition to his current account balance, then he must arrange, when the extractions are repaid, to ensure that the credits are made to each account to obtain the maximum relief under Section 419(4).

A less obvious liability may arise under Section 419(5). The subsection states:

> Where, under arrangements made by any person otherwise than in the ordinary course of a business carried on by him:
> (a) a close company makes a loan or advance which, apart from this subsection, does not give rise to any charge on the company under subsection (1) above, and
> (b) some person other than the close company makes a payment or transfers property to, or releases or satisfies (in whole or in part) a liability of an individual who is a participator in the company or an associate of a participator, then, unless in respect of the matter referred to in paragraph (b) above there fails to be included in the total income of the participator or associate an amount not less than the loan or advance, this section shall apply as if the loan or advance had been made to him.

This subsection would apply if, for instance, a director and participator in two companies arranged for one company to make a loan or advance to the second company, so that the second company could repay a loan to the director that it could not otherwise have repaid. This type of situation is only likely to arise when it is desired to supply a company which is indebted to a director with the funds to repay the director.

Section 109 TMA1970 brings Section 419 within the general provisions which apply to corporation tax. The section states:

(1) The provisions of Section 419 of the principal Act (charge of tax in connection with loans by close companies to participators etc.) directing that tax be assessed and recoverable as if it were an amount of corporation tax shall be taken as applying, subject to the provisions of the Taxes Acts, and to any necessary modifications, all enactments applying generally to corporation tax, including those relating to assessing, collecting and receiving of corporation tax, those conferring or regulating a right of appeal and those concerning administration, penalties, interest on unpaid tax and priority of tax in cases of insolvency under the law of any part of the United Kingdom.

(2) Section 86 of this Act shall apply in relation to tax under the said Section 419 as if the date given by the Table in subsection (4) of the said Section 86 were the last day of the three months following the end of the financial year in which the loan or advance was made.

(3) For the purposes of Section 88 of this Act as applied by subsection (1) above, the date when tax charged under the said Section 419 ought to have been paid shall be taken to be the first day of the financial year following that in which the loan or advance was made.

Obtaining Information in Company Cases

Difficulty has been experienced in company cases when it comes to obtaining particulars and documents from directors in connection with the taxation affairs of a company. The easiest way out of the dilemma is to assess both the directors and the company, and to obtain any necessary precepts from the Commissioners addressed to the company and or to one or more of its directors as appropriate in connection with their respective appeals. In fact, the company's accounts review is carried out in conjunction with the personal reviews of the directors' affairs, the object being to identify the weakest link in their joint affairs and activities.

It is not unknown for directors to keep their taxation affairs as separate from the company as possible, to discourage any Revenue investigation. The file of the company is normally dealt with by the District in whose area the registered office of the company is situated, while the directors' files are usually held in the District dealing with the main trade premises of the company from which the payment of wages etc. is made. This may mean that different, and geographically widely separated, tax offices deal with the affairs of the company and those of the directors. In addition, separate bodies of Commissioners may be involved in dealing with the respective corporation tax and Sch.E appeals. A further complication may be added by the making of alternative appeals to the General and to the Special Commissioners, with a view to still further fragmenting the Revenue's investigation and appeals procedures. Such ploys undoubtedly cause a considerable amount of extra effort by the Revenue in successfully completing any investigation, but the obstacles are not insurmountable and have been overcome in the past. Nevertheless, it would take a brave Inspector, acting on very good information, to begin to sort out such a case – one which is likely to play havoc with district targets. However, the artificial way in which the company's and the directors' affairs had been separated would stimulate unwelcome interest in such a wily bunch. It would be less obvious if the accountants engaged as the company's auditors had the registered office plate at their address and the accountants chosen had their affairs dealt with by a different tax office to that dealing with the business address of the company. In this way you could, if you desired, ensure that the accountants' address falls within the area of a different Division of Commissioners to that dealing with the business premises, and that the same Clerk is not employed to act for all of the Divisions concerned.

Section 44 TMA1970 sets out details of the Commissioners who should deal with appeals and other proceedings. The section was amended by Section 133 FA1988, that provides for the Board to be able to direct that 'proceedings before the General Commissioners under the Taxes Acts of any description specified in the direction should be brought before the General Commissioners for the division so specified in relation to proceedings of that description'. Therefore, the Board now have the power to direct that, notwithstanding the rules in Schedule 3 of the TMA1970, the Board may make a direction specifying the division of the General Commissioners who shall hear a particular case. This appears to be a tidying up exercise in relation to the General Commissioners, who may be given jurisdiction in any particular case.

There are other special legal niceties applying to companies. I do not propose to go into these matters in detail, apart from to note that monies have to be received by a company before they become company property, and that the theft of company monies does not confer the ownership of them on the thief. Therefore, in certain circumstances, there may be a technical defence against Schedule E assessments raised on directors in respect of alleged company monies or profits extracted by a director. However such issues may only be raised on appeal against the Schedule E assessments concerned. Moreover, Commissioners tend to be concerned with the intrinsic merits or otherwise of a taxpayer's case and are not likely to be impressed by the sort of arguments that would have to be advanced. Furthermore, they would be likely to issue precepts for the particulars and documents necessary to establish the case against the company or the director – and this particular ploy is unlikely to be either attractive or cost-effective.

The enquiry into the directors' affairs will cover such items as undeclared interest chargeable under Case III of Schedule D in addition to the question of extractions from the company, and other benefits and expense allowances chargeable on the director etc. Therefore, in a company case it is not unusual for separate settlements to be made with each of the directors and the company, with separate letters of offer in each case.

Although the Revenue considers that company extractions may be assessed directly on the directors, it is more usual to assess the company in respect of the understated profits. The exception arises in cases where the company is devoid of funds or assets and can be put into liquidation to avoid its responsibilities. The company could of course be put into Receivership and the Receiver could attempt to recover company monies retained by the directors. It is, however, more straightforward in such circumstances to assess all the extractions on the directors, and to seek direct payments from them of the tax, interest and penalties appropriate to the case. If the company is assessed in respect of the additional income then, at the conclusion of the enquiry, an undertaking will be sought to have the directors' loan and/or current accounts rewritten to take into account the extractions made by the directors. Subsequent accounts should then show the revised loan/current account balances flowing from the transactions in the current year. In this way the directors' loan/current accounts reflect all the transactions appropriate to those accounts.

Private or Company Transactions?

It should be remembered that companies are separate legal entities: confusion may arise when directors do not follow the strict demarcation appropriate to company and private transactions. A vehicle purchased by a direcler in his own name, out of his own funds, may be treated by him in the company records as a purchase by the company. Similarly, the insurance policy for the vehicle may be registered in his name. In such circumstances the Inspector may claim that the vehicle had incorrectly been shown as a company asset when all the documentation points to it being a private purchase by the director. A claim could be made that the vehicle was purchased on behalf of the company and no doubt the cost price would be credited to the director's loan/current account. However, it is better not to blur the edges between company and director: company transactions should pass through the company's bank account and any vehicles should be registered in the company's name. Clearly there could be insurance difficulties if the vehicle was only insured by the director, and no doubt the documentation would suggest that the vehicle was in the director's ownership. Such complications are quite unnecessary and should be avoided. If a director uses his or her vehicle for company purposes, a completely different set of statutory provisions apply both to the company and to the director. The director may claim capital allowances and vehicle expenses in respect of the wholly exclusive and necessary use of the vehicle in the performance of his professional duties. The company cannot claim the capital allowances in respect of the vehicle but may deduct the expenses payments to the director in its accounts. The director in turn will be assessed on the expenses payments, regardless of whether or not he may be able to claim that some, or all, were incurred wholly, exclusively and necessarily in the performance of his duties. It is normally more advantageous to have all the capital allowances allowed to the company, and the director assessed on the scale benefit charge in respect of the use of the company's vehicle. Therefore, it is not a good idea to suggest by your actions that a different treatment is more appropriate.

Some directors have been unwise enough to use their personal bank accounts for company purchases and expenses rather than, if necessary, introducing funds directly into the company's bank account, and then drawing cheques for company expenses on the company account. If you use your personal account for company purposes, you emphasise the close link between the company's and your private activities. You also make it very difficult for the book-keeper to identify all the transactions involved. Invoices kept with personal papers may be mislaid, and if the accountant is not made aware of the position and given your private bank statements etc. to include with the company records when carrying out his audit, the transactions can be overlooked altogether. If this happens, the company's accounts will be incorrect and the company's profit overstated for corporation tax purposes.

If the private bank statements are examined by an Inspector, company transactions are likely to be spotted. If they have not been dealt with properly in the accounts, the Inspector has good evidence to support a claim that the company's records are incomplete and the accounts incorrect. If the transactions are not spotted, the debits will tend to inflate the private expenditure figures – and that may be most unhelpful.

These strictures regarding mixing business and private transactions apply to all business activities, whether carried on by companies, individuals or partnerships.

11   Penalties

If, as in most cases, the Revenue investigation is to end in a monetary settlement, it will consist of an offer to pay a negotiated amount – either in a lump sum, or in instalments. The amount offered will have to cover the tax outstanding up to a specified date. The tax involved may be divided into two classifications:

1. culpable tax arising from any offences alleged to have occurred, that are specified offences in the Taxation Acts;
2. non-culpable tax being the tax arising on correctly and timeous declared income, and capital gains etc. that is unpaid at the date of the offer, in respect of the period covered by the offer.

The offer will also include interest exigible on the culpable tax under Section 88 TMA1970 and on the non-culpable tax under Section 86 up to the anticipated date of the letter of offer. There will be a further amount included in respect of the penalties claimed to have been incurred. The penalties will be the statutory penalties set out in the Taxation Acts in respect of the offences that are either agreed to have been committed by the taxpayer, or are alleged by the Revenue and are accepted by the taxpayer as being unlikely to be successfully disputed before the Commissioners.

There are a number of different acts of omission or commission that can give rise to statutory penalties. If the sections overlap giving rise to more than one tax-geared penalty, only one penalty is sought – but, you will not be surprised to learn, it is the largest of the penalties involved that is required (*see* S.97A TMA1970). The Board have the power to mitigate any penalties and interest as set out in the Taxation Acts, and it is due to these powers of the Board that negotiations take place. In practice, the interest charge is seldom reduced, and negotiations concentrate on the appropriate amount to be added for penalties – the penalty loading. The starting point, however, is the identification of the offences alleged to have been committed, the correct chargeable income, and the statutory penalties involved.

Penalties

Failure to Render a Return

A basic penalty provision, set out in Section 93 TMA1970 (as amended by S.162 FA1989) and applying to notices served on or after 6th April 1989, is concerned with the failure to comply with a notice to make a return for income tax, or capital gains tax. The initial penalty is an amount not exceeding £300: if the failure continues after the initial penalty has been imposed, there can be a further daily penalty not exceeding £60 for each day on which the failure continues. No penalty may be imposed under this section after the failure has been remedied (Section 93(5) TMA1970). If the failure continues after the end of the year of assessment following the year in which it was served, then without prejudice to the penalties already mentioned, you may be liable to an amount not exceeding the tax with which you are charged, for one, or more than one, year of assessment, based wholly or partly on any income or chargeable gains that ought to have been included in the return,. The tax involved, however, is only that assessed after the end of the year following the year in which the notice was served.

You will have to rely on the wording of the statute and the advice of your accountant but, broadly speaking, you may receive a 1991/92 return on or after 6th April 1991 calling for details of your income for 1990/91 (year ended 5th April 1991). You are given 30 days in which to complete the return. If you fail to complete the return, an officer of the Board may make a determination imposing a penalty (Section 100 TMA1970). Notice of a determination of a penalty will be served on the person liable, giving details of the time within which an appeal against the determination may be made. If the failure continues after the imposition of the initial penalty, a determination may be made for further penalties.

It is inadvisable to become involved in such procedures. Even if, at the end of the day, you prove that there was no income or chargeable gain to be included in the return, you can still face a penalty of up to £100. Prior to FA1989, the penalty could not exceed £5 – obviously Government opinion has hardened against taxation offences. It is simply not worth playing 'chicken' with the taxman. Work to a proper timetable, with the assistance of your accountant if necessary, but make sure your returns are submitted *on time*. If you have good reason for delaying the submission of a complete return, send in the partly completed return, with a letter of explanation stating that the remainder of the return details are to follow. It always pays to keep the Inspector informed of the cause of any delays, and to ensure that he does not feel either neglected or ignored.

It should be noted that under the provisions of Section 100(1) (as amended by S.167 FA1989), the officer of the Board may set the penalty at an amount he feels to be correct or appropriate. The penalty cannot be altered except where:

● the relevant amount of tax taken into account is, or has become, excessive:
● the amount of the penalty is varied on appeal against the determination of the penalty.

Under Section 100(c) (S.167 FA1989) proceedings may still be taken before the General of Special Commissioners in respect of penalties arising under Section 93(1) before its amendment by Section 162 FA1989 – i.e. notices served prior to 6 April 1989. The penalties for the late delivery of corporation tax returns are set out in Section 94 TMA1970 as amended by Section 83FA(No2)1987. The penalties for failure to deliver a return and so on within the time limits specified are avoidable with the minimum of effort. Do not neglect your tax affairs, or allow your accountant to neglect them: it is expensive and unproductive.

Incorrect Returns
Section 95 TMA1970 imposes penalties where a person fraudulently of negligently delivers an incorrect return for income tax or capital gains tax. A penalty is also set for any incorrect claim for any allowance, deduction or relief, in respect of income tax or capital gains tax, or for the submission of any incorrect accounts relating to his liability to those taxes. The amount of the penalty has been amended by Section 163 FA1989 in respect of returns, statements, declarations or accounts delivered, made or submitted on or after 27 July 1989. The current penalty is an amount not exceeding the difference between the amount of income tax and capital gains tax payable for the relevant years of assessment and the amount which would have been payable if the returns had been correct.

The relevant years of assessment are, in relation to anything delivered, made or submitted in any year of assessment:

● that year;
● the next following;
● the preceding year of assessment.

Therefore, the penalty cannot exceed the amount of the tax lost due to the incorrect return etc. It must be stressed, however, that this is a penalty and is levied *in addition* to the correct amount of tax due.

Prior to FA1989 the penalty in the case of fraud was twice the amount of the difference between the correct amount of tax and that based on the incorrect return. In practice, the maximum penalty loading was not sought by the Board, so the amendment does not indicate a softening of the Board's attitude to fraud cases. Similar provisions apply to incorrect returns for corporation tax, dealt with in Section 96 TMA1970 (as amended by S.163 FA1989). It is under the provisions of Sections 95 and 96 that the majority of penalties arise.

If an incorrect return etc. is made or submitted neither fraudulently nor negligently, and the error comes to the notice of the person concerned (or if he has died, to the attention of his personal representatives), unless it is remedied without unreasonable delay, the return etc. will be treated as having been negligently made or submitted. It must also be noted that any accounts submitted on behalf of another person are deemed to have been submitted by him, unless he can prove that they were submitted without his consent or connivance (S.97 TMA1970). It is for this reason that your accountant retains a copy of your formal approval of your accounts for submission to the Revenue.

Failure to Notify Chargeability

In the past, the cheapest way to evade tax, from a penalty point of view, was simply not to join the system: failure to notify liability to income tax and corporation tax attracted a maximum penalty of £100 only for each of the years involved, prior to FA1988. With the passing of the 1988 FA, however, the failure offence, with respect to notices required to be given for 1988/89 for income tax and, for accounting periods ending after 31 March 1989 for corporation tax, were put on a more level footing with the penalties for failing to submit returns. In the case of income tax, the penalty is an amount not exceeding the amount of the tax for which the taxpayer is liable, in respect of income from that source for that year, due under assessments made more than twelve months after the end of that year. The same principle applies to corporation tax. The relevant statutory provisions are contained in Sections 7 and 10 of the TMA1970. A new Section, 11A, was enacted in FA1988 to include the requirement to give notice of chargeability to capital gains tax for 1988/89 onwards.

You may put yourself into a penalty position if you:

- fail to give notice of chargeability to tax;
- fail to deliver a return, etc.;
- deliver an incorrect return, etc.

Any person who either assists in or induces the preparation or delivery of any information, return, account or other document, which he knows to be incorrect, and which are likely to be used for any tax purpose, is liable to a penalty not exceeding £3,000. Prior to the passing of Section 166 FA1989 the penalty was a derisory maximum of £500: again it is clear that the Government is 'firming up' the penalties for evading tax. It also explains why your accountant, professional and moral ethics apart, is not likely to wish to become involved in anybody's machinations. Proceedings for a penalty under Section 99 TMA1970 (as amended by S.166 FA1989) may be begun before a court at any time within *20 years* after the date on which the penalty was incurred.

Time Limits

The next thing to consider is the number of years for which assessments may be made and penalties imposed. Under the provision of Section 36 TMA1970 (as amended by S.149 FA1989) an assessment may be made on any person for the purpose of making good to the Crown a loss of tax attributable to his fraudulent or negligent conduct (or that of a person acting on his behalf) at any time not later than 20 years after the end of the chargeable period to which the assessment relates. This is extended under sub-paragraph(2) to include an individual who traded in partnership with another individual, or with other persons – i.e. companies – provided that at least one of the others involved was an individual. Such assessments may be made not only on the person in default, but also on his partner who is an individual.

The Inspector will proceed to establish the penalty position by making 'a discovery' to enable him to make additional assessments for the purpose of recovering tax lost due to your alleged failure to fulfil your obligation to produce information required under the Taxes Acts. Alternatively, the assessments may be made to recover tax lost due to an error in any information delivered to an Inspector.

The let-out clause in Section 118(2) allowed a person with a reasonable excuse for not fulfilling a requirement to be deemed not to have failed to do it – if he did it without unreasonable delay after the excuse had ceased. This is specifically excluded by Section 88(7) (S.159 FA1989). So no failure can be effectively remedied for Section 88 interest purposes.

The determination of any appeals against additional assessments, either by formal agreement with the Inspector in writing, or on the determination of the appeals by the Commissioners, will finalise the amount of the assessments. Section 101 TMA1970 provides that any assessment that can no longer be varied by any Commissioners on appeal, or by order of any court, shall be sufficient evidence that the income, or chargeable gains in respect of which tax is charged in the assessment, arose, or were received as stated therein. The Inspector may

Penalties

then proceed to issue a notice of a determination under Section 88 to be served on the taxpayer, specifying:

- the date of issue of the determination;
- the amount of the tax which carried interest identifying the assessments concerned;
- the date when, for the purposes of Section 88, the tax ought to have been paid;
- the time within which an appeal against the determination may be made.

The notice of determination cannot be altered except on appeal to the Commissioners who may vary or set it aside, or confirm it. The Section 88 interest position will then be finally determined and any tax carrying interest under Section 88 will not carry interest under Section 86 (S.88(3) as amended by S.161 FA1989).

A determination under Section 88 may be made at any time within six years of the chargeable period for which the tax carrying the interest is charged, or within three years after the date of the final determination of the assessments involved.

As has been noted, an officer of the Board, authorised by the Board, may make a determination imposing a penalty under any provision of the Taxes Acts, setting it at an amount which, in his opinion, is correct or appropriate (S.100(1) TMA1970 as amended by S.167 FA1989). Notice of a determination of a penalty will be served on the taxpayer, stating the date of issue and the time limit within which an appeal against it may be made. Where the penalised person has died, the liability arising from the deceased' actions, falls on his personal representatives, and any penalty imposed becomes a debt of the estate.

Any appeal will be dealt with by the Commissioners in basically the same way as an appeal against an assessment. If it appears to them that no penalty has been incurred, they may set aside the determination: if the amount of the penalty appears to them to be correct, they may confirm it. They also have the power to increase or decrease the penalty to the amount they judge to be correct. An appeal from a decision of the Commissioners against the amount of a penalty determined by them lies at the instance of the person liable to the penalty and goes to the High Court – or in Scotland, the Court of Session.

Penalty Proceedings

Penalty proceedings must still be brought before the General of Special Commissioners in respect of penalties incurred for failing to comply with notices served on or before 5 April 1989 under Section 100(2)

111

TMA1970 (as amended by S.167 FA1989) without any prior determination by the authorised officer. The proceedings are by way of information in writing, made to the Commissioners by the Inspector, and upon a summons issued by the Commissioners to the taxpayer. An appeal again goes to the High Court or the Court of Session in Scotland. The appeal may only be, by either party, on a question of law, or by the taxpayer against the amount of the penalty (S.100c TMA1970).

Where, in the opinion of the Board, the liability of any person for a penalty arises by reason of fraud, proceedings for the penalty may be instituted before the High Court (in Scotland, the Court of Session) (S.100D TMA1970). Penalty proceedings may be commenced:

- at any time within six years after the date on which the penalty was incurred, or
- at any later time within three years after the determination of the amount of the tax by reference to which the amount of the penalty is to be ascertained.

Where the tax was payable by a person who has died, the second case above does not apply if the tax was charged in an assessment made later than six years after the end of the chargeable period for which it was charged (S.103 TMA1970).

So the Inspector can take action to have appeals against the assessments determined, issue a notice of determination under s.88 in respect of the interest on the culpable tax, and make or have made, a determination of the penalties, with the alternative of instituting penalty proceedings before the Commissioners (or in the case of fraud, in the High Court). Now for the good news: the procedures outlined will only be followed when the Inspector finds it impossible to negotiate a reasonable settlement with you. Under Section 102 TMA1970:

'The Board may in their discretion mitigate any penalty, or stay or compound any proceedings for the recovery thereof, and may also, after judgement, further mitigate or entirely remit the penalty'.

They are unlikely to mitigate the interest charge under Section 88 because that charge is considered by the Board to represent fair commercial restitution for having been deprived of the use of the additional tax claimed for the period of the enquiry up to the date of settlement.

I must also emphasise that the procedures introduced by FA1989 are relatively new. I do not believe that it is envisaged that large numbers of cases will find their way to the Commissioners for determination. The outcome of such procedures would be likely to vary very markedly, at least initially, until the Commissioners established the going rates for the different types of offences with which they were dealing. There may be a lot of huffing and puffing on each side, but at the end of the day you would be foolish to insist on going through all the legal procedures, rather than doing a deal with the local Inspector. Get the best deal you can, and if you think that the facts and evidence warrant it, fight the amount of the additional assessments made – but leave the rest to negotiations with the Inspector. You may, if necessary, ask his Head Office to review the papers, if you consider he is being unreasonable.

Special Returns

Separate penalty provisions deal with special returns, etc. as specified in Section 98 TMA1970. I do not propose to go into detail on this subject as any such returns will display information concerning the statutory penalties for failing to comply with the notice. There is an initial penalty of an amount not exceeding £300 and a follow-up penalty of up to £60 per day. If you supply incorrect information, either fraudulently or negligently, the penalty may rise to £3,000. A number of other penalties have been similarly up-rated. It is advisable, therefore, to give all statutory notices from the Revenue the time and consideration they warrant.

Penalty Section 98A TMA1970 (introduced by S.165 FA1989), takes the profit out of failing to make a return under the PAYE regulations and sub-contractors' legislation. Again I do not propose to go into detail of this but merely wish to draw your attention to this legislation.

Section 20 of the TMA1970 has been amended by Sections 142 and 168 FA1989 and enlarged by the addition of sub-sections 20BB and 20CC: the additions and amendments covering nine pages of print. The section is concerned with the power to call for documents of a taxpayer from various persons including banks and accountants, as are in that person's possession or power, and may contain information relevant to any tax liability (or to the amount of such liability) to which the taxpayer is, or may be, subject. It is again indicative of the strength of Government feeling on combating the evasion of tax by persons who do not willingly co-operate with Revenue enquiries. In this connection, under Section 20BB it is an offence if a person intentionally falsifies, conceals, destroys or otherwise disposes of (or causes or permits such actions) a document which has been required by a Section 20 notice, or has been given an opportunity by a Section 20B notice to deliver or make available for inspection the items required. When it comes to the loss or destruction of a document, the crux of the matter is the word 'intentionally'. One can envisage the employment of inadequate or poorly-instructed staff for instance, who misinterpret their duties and inadvertently destroy relevant documents. It would also seem a complete answer to show that the documents had been disposed of prior to the issue of the Section 20 order. However, since items being sought are in the power, possession or control of persons outside the *direct* influence of the taxpayer, the danger of 'inadvertent' destruction of essential documents is limited.

Under Section 20C, a warrant may be obtained to enable Revenue officers to enter premises and seize documents if they can satisfy a Circuit Judge, Sheriff or, in Northern Ireland, a County Court Judge that such action is justified. This section is only employed in the most extreme cases, but it must be pointed out that documents seized could give rise to enquiries into other taxpayers' affairs.

Gathering Information
There are a number of returns that can be required by the Inspector that are directly concerned with gathering information about other taxpayers' affairs. The basic ones are:

- Section 13 TMA1970. Details from persons in receipt of taxable income belonging to others of the names and addresses of the persons to whom the income belongs, and the respective amounts involved.
- Section 14 TMA1970. Details from persons having lodgers or inmates resident in their houses of the name, and the ordinary place of residence if resident elsewhere.
- Section 16 TMA1970. Details from traders of the fees and commissions for services by persons not employed in the trade or business. This section applies to payments from 1988/89 onwards by any depart- ment of the Crown, any public or local authority, and any other public body.
- Section 17 TMA1970. Details of interest paid or credited by banks, etc. without the deduction of tax, stating the name and address of the recipient.
- Section 18 TMA1970. Details of the interest paid without deduction of income tax by any person, stating the name and address of the recipient and the amount involved.
- Section 18A TMA1970. Details of any payment out of public funds by way of grant or subsidy, stating the name and address of the recipient and the amount involved.
- Any person by whom licences or approvals are issued or a register maintained may be required to supply details of any person who is, or has been, the holder of a licence or approval issued to whom an entry in the register relates. This section does not apply to a payment made, or to a licence, approval or entry which ceased either before

6 April 1988, or in a year of assessment ending more than three years before the date of giving the notice.

Again the sharpening up of the provisions that can require information about the activities of other taxpayers, and the income being derived from the various sources is indicative of the Government's resolve to bear down on tax evasion. For a number of years Revenue officers have been seeking information informally and, while those activities will no doubt continue, there is now a clear attempt to bring marginal items within the statutory field, so that information can be required, rather than requested on a grace and favour basis.

There are additional sections requiring information for the purposes of Schedule A (Section 19), stock jobbers transactions (Section 21), power to obtain details of income from securities (Section 23), and chargeable gains (Sections 25 and 27). The list is not exhaustive but gives you some idea of how wide the Revenue net may be cast. However, the Revenue must be selective in the information they require and be cost effective in their activities. Nevertheless, the Revenue hold considerable powers should they be needed.

The penalty provisions specified in Section 98 relate to the various returns referred to above and also apply to failing to comply with the requirements of a Commissioner's precept.

The whole of the anti-evasion legislation is geared to collecting information from third parties, with a view to establishing that taxpayers' accounts and returns are incorrect or incomplete. The sections then divide between those concerned with the semi-routine collection and dissemination of information to individual taxpayer's records, and the more precisely targeted requests for information where co-operation is not forthcoming, or where there is reason to believe that serious fraud is involved. The future may well bring a harmonization of the collection and possible exchange of information within the EC, as taxation fraud crosses national boundaries.

For the normal taxpayer all the complex sections and procedures count for very little, unless he is intent on trying to buck the system and comes unstuck. The general taxpayer need only know that he should comply with any notices served on him within the time limits specified and that, if he understates or omits items of chargeable income from his accounts or returns, he may have to pay a penalty, based on a percentage of the tax lost due to his neglect. He will, of course, have to also pay interest to the Revenue to recompense the Board for the late payment of the culpable tax.

The Revenue, thanks to the march of progress, now have computers and these may be used to store information on taxpayers, gleaned from various returns and other sources of information. Therefore, there will be less chance of little gems of information being lost or overlooked. However, under the Data Protection Act, any taxpayer may see a copy of all the information held on Revenue computers concerning his affairs. This is an advantage since the information held may be incorrect or misleading. Although such applications are not yet common, it will be interesting to see whether or not they become so – and the effect that they may have on Revenue procedures for keeping any potentially sensitive information on computer file. The possibility of taxpayers exercising their rights and asking for details of the information stored on Revenue computers every year, before they complete their tax returns, is an option for any taxpayer. However, such action may attract undue attention, the Inspector no doubt being curious about the cause for the taxpayer's anxiety.

I am not saying that you cannot win – simply that it is difficult not to lose!

12 The Offer

The letter of offer, to be a legally binding contract, must offer a valuable consideration in respect of the payment. The Inspector is given guidance by his Head Office concerning the wording and layout considered to be appropriate by the Board for the offer. The letter of offer is addressed to the Commissioners of Inland Revenue, and contains a specific acceptance that an offence has been committed that renders the taxpayer liable to penalties and interest in respect of the duty, i.e. the tax specified in the schedule that forms part of the letter of offer. The schedule will specify year by year, or accounting period by accounting period, for each duty involved – i.e. income tax, capital gains tax or corporation tax – and the amount agreed to be due. If non- culpable duty is included, it will be specifically mentioned. The last thing the Board wants is for there to be any ambiguity about what is covered by the letter of offer. The letter of offer is normally signed by the taxpayer making the offer. In the case of a company, it should be signed by the company secretary and the directors, and should carry the company seal to make the offer fully binding on the company.

Although the Board have a preferred format for the letter of offer, there is no statutory layout or terminology which must be followed. It is, for instance, sufficient for the taxpayer to say 'whereby it is alleged that tax has been lost due to my fraudulent or negligent conduct' rather than 'whereby tax has been lost due to my fraudulent or negligent conduct'. Such a change in the normally preferred wording would only be acceptable where there had indeed been no specific admission by the taxpayer of identified taxation offences. All the taxpayer is conceding is that, because of the peculiar circumstances of his case and the heavy onus of proof that he has to discharge, he can accept that the Revenue may make out a case for the additional assessments that could be invloved, and that he is unlikely to be able to satisfy the Commissioners that any such assessments are excessive. This distinction may seem a rather fine one to the taxpayer required to find a substantial sum to settle the Revenue claims, however, it is a very real and important distinction. In the second case there is a clear admission that the Revenue can sustain a claim that an offence has been committed – and you are admitting

117

your guilt. However, by the insertion of 'alleged' in the first case you are making no such admission, effectively saying that though the Revenue case may be strong it is unproved: the Revenue have made allegations and payment is made in the light of those allegations, without any specific admission of guilt.

The letter of offer will refer to any payments already made on account, and specify a time limit for payment of the balance of the sum offered in settlement of the tax lost, interest and penalties. There is also provision in the letter of offer for further interest to accrue if payment of the sum offered is not made within the time limit stipulated, normally within 30 days of the date of the letter confirming acceptance of the offer by the Inspector.

In some instances taxpayers simply cannot bring themselves to admit openly and without equivocation that they have been guilty of a Revenue offence. In other cases, the legally minded are too wary to burn their boats and make a specific admission. While the matter is still one of conjecture, even though the circumstantial evidence is overwhelming, judicious clinging to a defensible if unlikely position may be sufficient to put a taxpayer in a better bargaining position than one making a frank admission of his guilt. You could draw an analogy between the taxpayer's position *vis à vis* the Inspector to the plea bargaining common in the American judicial system. Once guilt is admitted, there is nothing to bargain with on behalf of the accused to get the best deal available. The scales of justice are quite heavily damped by the perceived need for expediency. The Board is clearly anxious to demonstrate (by reference to the Department's statistics) that they are meeting their targets for investigation settlements. They have no personal interest in the amounts extracted from individual taxpayers. The individual cases are not reported publicly anywhere, whether settled by agreement on appeal or by penalty proceedings before Commissioners – and no publicity means that there is no knock-on deterrent value. The circumstances of each case are covered by Section 182 FA1989 and cannot be divulged to anyone outside the Inland Revenue department. The taxpayer may well keep quiet about the Revenue investigation and the eventual settlement. On the other hand he may tell a pack of lies to his cronies about how he pulled the wool over the Inspector's eyes and still made a 'profit' from his extractions. He may actually have succeeded in doing just that, but who is to know the truth in such a case where the taxpayer is a stranger to the truth in the first place?

The Taxpayer's Quandary
The Board will wish to have a balanced view taken of the evidence and proceed accordingly. The Board acts through its appointees and they,

being career civil servants, will not wish to rock the boat or cause a stir without very good justification. Judicious brinkmanship is, therefore, the order of the day if you wish to avoid having to expend your energy, and probably quite a lot of money, in disputing the Revenue claims formally before the Commissioners. The question no doubt uppermost in most taxpayers' minds is, are they going to win at the end of the day? To answer that question they must first consider who they are fighting and just what winning means to them. Personalities should not enter into the equation and there should be no personal animosity towards the Inspector, who is only attempting to carry out his duties. The manner in which the Inspector conducts the investigation may well give rise to antagonism but such feelings are usually centred on the expected outcome of the investigation – that is, the Inspector is likely to ask for a sizeable slice, if not all, of your accumulated wealth. The resentment and personalizing of the investigation generally starts with the taxpayer and clouds his judgement. The taxpayer may be abusive and thoroughly objectionable but being a civil servant, the Inspector must be correct at all times – whatever the cost to his blood pressure. The conflict may become quite bitter and counterproductive, with the taxpayer airing his displeasure while the Inspector can only translate his suppressed anger into an ever greater resolve to leave no stone unturned, and not to allow the taxpayer to get away with anything. Anger is a strong motivating force and the Inspector in such circumstances is likely to redouble his personal input into the case and, by virtue of the expenditure of his time will eventually have to seek a larger overall settlement to justify the time allocated to the case. This scenario is somewhat exaggerated, but the underlying principle is valid. Do not have personal conflicts with the Inspector: patiently and clearly argue your point of view on any disagreements about the interpretation to be placed on the facts established and the inferences to be drawn from them. Set out your own position clearly and unequivocally to strengthen your own case, and do not accept any assertions of the Inspector that are detrimental to your position without challenge and response.

The Certificate of Full Disclosure

At the offer stage, the negotiations of the understated or omitted income will be over. You will have been asked to complete a certificate of full disclosure that is linked to a certified statement of assets at a date at or around the enquiry termination date. The certificate of full disclosure is not a statutory requirement although its request by the Board has received the support of the courts. Taxpayers are entitled to argue that their Capital, Income and Expenditure Statements have been adopted by them prior to their submission to the Revenue and so no further statement should be necessary. However, the Inspector is accustomed to asking for such a certificate as part of normal departmental procedure and will not abandon the request lightly. Indeed, Inspectors have faithfully obtained the completion of certificates of full disclosure that specify a period (normally the full period of the enquiry) to which they are supposed to relate when they have never sought, let alone obtained, all the details specified on the certificate that they have requested. The result has been quite useless, invalid certificates which have been dutifully filed away in the taxpayer's papers awaiting the day when the Inspector can establish that a full disclosure was not made by the date of the conclusion of the enquiry!

The Amount to be Offered
Returning to the offer, when the Inspector is satisfied that the taxpayer has made a full disclosure and has made specific admission or at least tacit acceptance that irregularities have taken place, he will seek to compute the amount of the expected offer. The idea is to indicate to the taxpayer the amount of the offer that, in all the circumstances of the taxpayer's case, is likely to be acceptable to the Board. The Inspector will normally seek an interview with the taxpayer to outline his thinking on the penalty position. It must be clear, however, that penalties are stated to be amounts not exceeding specific sums computed by reference to the tax lost and the number of incorrect or late returns, etc. The Board have attempted to formulate a way in which to arrive at a penalty that would be acceptable to them in exercising their powers to mitigate penalties. However, cases are so diverse that interpretation of the Board's instructions may vary from district to district, and be coloured by the personalities involved. It is, therefore, quite impossible to say that any particular amount is the only amount that would be accepted by the Board in any specific case. It must also be noted that the Board's internal instructions and assumptions about how to arrive at the appropriate penalty level in any particular case are not binding on the General Commissioners or the Courts before whom any appeal proceedings may be taken. This is a very grey area, and one in which you should give yourself the benefit of the doubt. If the Inspector is building his case on shifting sand, where nothing is positively admitted, where conclusions are built on inferences drawn from the few sparse facts available, and where those inferences have been the subject of dispute, the Inspector will be less inclined to be pedantic about the precise penalty loading percentages appropriate to the case.

You may also anticipate that the Inspector will make pragmatic decisions based on the availability of funds and that the amount of understatements agreed, the resulting tax loss, and overall penalty sought may reflect the taxpayer's ability to actually pay the amount considered appropriate to the case – everyone is aware that you cannot get blood out of a stone. This does not mean, however, that the Inspector will have no room to manoeuvre: his demands may eventually go well beyond the taxpayer's means to fund a settlement. Indeed, circumstances may dictate that the Inspector will have to proceed by way of formalised assessments and interest certificates and so on, leaving any collection problems in the hands of the Collector of Taxes.

Inadequate Funds

You should be aware that the collection of taxes is dealt with by a separate branch of the Inland Revenue. Once the Inspector of Taxes has established the legal validity of the tax charge and obtained an interest certificate, attention can be paid to the advisability of instituting penalty proceedings. If the taxpayer would be bankrupted by the tax charge alone, the necessity for further action beyond the determination of the assessments may not be considered appropriate. Having established the charge on the taxpayer the Inspector may close his enquiry leaving the Collector to pursue the taxpayer – through the courts if necessary – to recover the money due to the Revenue.

Immediate lack of funds may not be a bar to obtaining a satisfactory offer. If the taxpayer is engaged in a thriving business he may be expected to seek financial assistance from his bank, for example, to fund a settlement. There could also be the question of using personal as well as business assets to secure advances to fund a settlement. In company cases the Revenue may consider the directors funding the company settlement, at least to the extent necessary to put their loan/current accounts in credit, and to obtain the benefit of any repayment or set-offs due under the provisions of Section 419(4). The elimination of the Section 419 tax is, of course, very desirable and would normally assist in reducing the offer figure to a more acceptable level.

If funds are not immediately available to finance a settlement the Board may be prepared to enter into an instalment offer agreement whereby the amount offered in settlement is paid over a period of time rather than in a lump sum. The terms of such an offer, however, take into account an additional interest element to compensate for the delayed payment involved. The terms of the offer normally state that on any default the remainder of the amount due under the instalment agreement becomes payable immediately.

It may be appropriate to mention here that it is not unknown for taxpayers to breathe a sigh of relief at the conclusion of the enquiry, and to pay the sum offered to the Revenue out of funds not disclosed during the course of the enquiry. Naïve though this may seem, it has happened – just as some taxpayers have, in a fit of nervous confusion, sent in the 'other' set of books (i.e. those showing the correct sales figures) when asked for their business records. Some taxpayers have contrived to adjust company records so that amounts advanced to directors to fund personal Revenue settlements have been shown as debts due from other companies. Beware: the Revenue are aware of such procedures and have met and dealt with them in the past.

Revenue Guidance

The Inland Revenue have issued a guidance leaflet IR 73 (available at any tax office) setting out in broad terms the way in which penalties may be mitigated by the Board to take into account various aspects of the investigation as perceived by the Inspector and recorded in his papers.

The first item to be considered is how the understatement of income came to light. The mitigation available to a taxpayer can be as high as 30 per cent for somebody who approaches the Revenue, at a time when they have no reason to believe that their transgressions will come to light, and makes a voluntary disclosure to the Revenue. If the taxpayer then fully and activity co-operates with the Revenue investigation into his voluntary disclosure, a further mitigation of up to 40 per cent may be allowed. Finally, consideration will be given to the gravity of the offences involved. A reduction of a further 40 per cent may accrue under the gravity heading. A little simple arithmetic will show you that it is theoretically possible to obtain a 110 per cent mitigation of penalties:

	%
Disclosure	30
Co-operation	40
Gravity	40
Total	110

I do not suggest that the Board will make a refund, or that you will receive any positive set-off against the tax bill. Therefore, on the face of it, you can afford to be 10 per cent naughty without incurring any extra cost – the whiter than white pay just the same as the plain white!

If you read the Revenue's leaflet IR 73 you will see that between the extremes there is considerable latitude when it comes to deciding the penalty loading appropriate to any particular case. Clearly it is advisable to consider the Board's published policy guidelines on the mitigation of penalties at the very outset of any Revenue enquiry.

Disclosure

Deciding on the disclosure category applicable may be difficult. If, for example, on challenge a taxpayer realises that he has been negligent in not disclosing some investment income and promptly discloses the source to the Inspector, on the face of it a mitigation factor of 20 per cent of the penalty could be appropriate. If the enquiry continues with the full co-operation of the taxpayer and an inconclusive picture emerges, the position may be more complicated. Does the taxpayer stick to his guns and say that there is nothing wrong, despite what other people in the area may be making from comparable businesses, or does he accept additions to his profit figure because he feels that, whatever the truth of the matter, he is fighting a lost cause and could lose valuable mitigation advantages by maintaining his innocence? The Revenue leaflet suggests that 'If you deny until the last possible moment that there is anything wrong, you will not get any reduction for disclosure at all'. Does this mean that a last minute admission will put you in the same position as somebody who denies irregularities, but who accepts that they are not in a position to produce lawful evidence to prove that the Inspector's figures are excessive? I suspect that it does, although it is possible that a taxpayer's only fault is that he is an incompetent businessman and he has got his books in a mess. Clearly such a result in the circumstances outlined would be unfair. However, Revenue is not concerned with abstract justice but with the facts of the case and the Inspector's evaluation of those facts. Essentially it may simply come down to a matter of the balance of probabilities on the evidence adduced during the course of the enquiry. It is up to the taxpayer to ensure that his business and private records will support his contentions, that his case is advanced in a cogent forceful manner, and that the Inspector's arguments are fully countered. Nothing should be left unanswered or unchallenged. However, if you find yourself unable to convince the Inspector that your accounts and so on are correct, and are not prepared or advised to take the appeals to the Commissioners, then you must anticipate that the Inspector will contend for a penalty without mitigation for disclosure. Working with the benefit of hindsight, a taxpayer may have been better advised to admit at the outset that something could be amiss, due to mess and muddle, and to use his accountant's report as a disclosure statement, thereby claiming at least some mitigation of penalties. In addition, the admission at an early stage may be beneficial enabling an early payment on account to be made and minimising interest build-up. Your accountant's fees may also be reduced by shortening the period between challenge and settlement, and, therefore, the work involved.

Co-operation

Closely following 'disclosure' is 'co-operation', with a penalty mitigation of up to 40 per cent on offer. Clearly, if the Inspector has to seek Commissioners' precepts for documents and/or particulars, or has to lay an information before Commissioners concerning your failure to render returns within the time allowed for their delivery, he will have clear evidence of your lack of co-operation. If you employ a dilatory accountant and there are long delays in dealing with correspondence, you can expect further black marks. The delays will be attributed to *you*, so it is up to you to ensure that your accountant is active in your cause and replying to the Inspector's letters. In their leaflet, the Revenue make the further point that if you 'avoid attending interviews' you will be penalised in the mitigation factor for co-operation. Just remember that the Board write their own rules when it comes to mitigation of penalties.

It can be argued that if a taxpayer has nothing to hide he should be happy to attend the Inspector's office and answer the Inspector's questions. Unfortunately, the Inspector's office is not the best place to question the propriety of the Inspector's questions or their relevance to your taxation affairs. Taxpayers tend to become nervous and flustered by the novel situation in which they find themselves and the personal information that may be requested. You will have no time to collect your thoughts on detailed explanations going back over a period of years. You may easily give honestly mistaken answers and then find that your incorrect answers are used to challenge your veracity as a witness, undermining your credibility. If you are going to attend the Inspector's office I suggest you do so *after* your accountant has carried out his detailed review of your affairs and you are both satisfied that the Inspector has valid grounds for challenging your accounts, etc. Let the Inspector state the grounds for his challenge in detail in the first instance, on the basis that until he has fully justified the need for an interview the costs involved in attending the Inspector's office with your accountant are an unnecessary and unwarranted expense. It is also open to your accountant to advise you that in his view particular questions put during the course of the interview should not be answered on the spot without further research. Your professional adviser is perfectly entitled to give such advice if he considers it appropriate in his client's interests. However, in my experience few professional advisers are of any practical assistance at interviews and, indeed, most seem to be mere spectators, acquiescing to whatever procedure the Inspector chooses to adopt. This, like so many aspects of an investigation, is a matter on which you should seek the best professional advice available. However, do remember to follow the professional advice you receive: do not abandon it because you think that you know best. If you know best, why pay out good money for advice that you are not going to follow?

The eventual adjustment for co-operation will effectively be a matter for negotiation and will be coloured by the degree of culpability established. The overall strength of the Inspector's case is likely to influence his degree of flexibility on penalties. If, for instance, off the record discussions between your accountant and the Inspector are possible,it might be found that the Inspector (for statistical purposes) would be more amenable to adjusting profit figures with a view to establishing what is, in his view, a more satisfactory penalty loading. Frank, off the record exchanges of views may be of the greatest assistance in smoothing the progress to a satisfactory settlement. If your accountant is at loggerheads with the Inspector such exchanges are likely to be more difficult and, if the Inspector feels that he has been let down by the accountant at some time in the past, such a procedure may not be acceptable to him.

The Gravity of the Offence

The third mitigation component is 'gravity' for which a further 40 per cent mitigation is available. The Revenue leaflet points to the nature of the way in which the offence has been perpetrated and organised as being aspects that will be taken into account, together with the period concerned and the amounts of money involved. They will also look at the nature of the offence in relation to the size of your business. The gravity of offences arising from mess and muddle as distinct from forgery and fraud are vastly different, although the quantum of the under-statement of the profits may be similar.

When the Revenue come to computing the penalty addition, the various statutory penalty maximums are largely ignored. The Inspector starts with a maximum figure of 100 per cent of the tax lost. From this figure he deducts the percentages considered to be appropriate for mitigation, for example:

		%	%
Penalty			100
Less	Disclosure	10	
	Co-operation	15	
	Gravity	20	45
Mitigated Penalty			55

125

The Inspector will then ensure that the proposed mitigated penalty addition of 55 per cent of the tax lost does not exceed the maximum statutory overall penalty for each of the offences alleged to have been committed. He will never knowingly seek a mitigated penalty larger than the statutory maximum.

There is no limitation on the Board's power to mitigate penalties so the way in which the law is formulated gives the Board *carte blanche*, subject to the overriding limit of the statutory penalties laid down in the Taxation Acts.

The General Commissioners and the Courts have no published guidelines on how they may reach a decision on the penalties they may consider appropriate in any particular case. Presumably some guidance is given, and perhaps notes are issued by the Lord Chancellor's Office to the General Commissioners in the same way that magistrates are assisted in laying down a similar range of penalties throughout the country for the same types of offence. No doubt the penalties involved will show the same capriciousness as those shown to be imposed on motorists when motoring organisations collect statistics to demonstrate the disparity in tariffs over the country. Therefore, listen to what the Inspector has to say about penalties, or get his views by telephone or letter. He should make it clear that he may only give guidance as to the level of penalties that he considers his instructions indicate are likely to be appropriate in your case. He has no statutory authority to reject any offer that you choose to make to the Board, neither may he accept any offer – although within certain limits the Board's powers are in practise delegated to the Inspector. In anticipation of a lower offer than he may feel is appropriate, the Inspector may pitch the mitigation factor rather low to allow perhaps ten per cent leeway between what he is saying is appropriate and the figure that he anticipates the taxpayer will actually offer on the advice of his accountant. The outcome is that while most offers made come in at a satisfactory level, some are too low and are referred back to the taxpayer to think again – in rare cases the taxpayer is actually advised that a lower offer would in fact be acceptable.

Pitching the offer at the right level is more of an art than a science. Go too low and the Inspector will have to make a detailed report to his Head Office setting out all the relevant facts. Head Office may decide that they should take the taxpayer to task for being cheeky and seek a marginally higher penalty loading than might otherwise have been accepted. It is a very delicate balancing act and to ensure that all the points that you wish to make in mitigation of the offences committed are fully and properly represented to the officer at Head Office, you should itemise them in a letter accompanying the letter of offer (see Fig. 12.1).

Figure 12.1 Specimen Letter of Offer

To the Commissioners of Inland Revenue

In consideration of no proceedings being taken against me in respect of the duties set out in the statement below, which I acknowledge and agree to be unpaid by reason, wholly or in part, of my default, or in respect of the penalties and interest to which I may thereby have become liable under the Taxes Acts, I _____ [name and address] hereby offer in respect of the said duties, penalties and interest, the sum of £___ (of which I have already paid £___ on account), to be paid within 30 days of the date of the letter notifying the acceptance of this offer by you. If the said sum has not been paid by the day specified herein then interest* shall be payable upon the said sum of £___ or any balance thereof at such rates as may from time to time be prescribed by the Taxes Acts for interest on overdue Income Tax, from that day.

Date _____ Signed _____

Statement of duties unpaid by me

Year	Nature of duty	Amount

* This interest is payable without deduction of Income tax.

Many letters of offer will have to be submitted by the Inspector to his Head Office for consideration, regardless of whether or not they apparently conform to the penalty limits indicated in the Inspector's instructions. In such cases any letter confirming acceptance of the offer may well come direct from the Head Office. If the offer is rejected the matter will normally be referred back through the District.

It cannot be emphasised too strongly how statistically conscious the

Inland Revenue is, and that there is a positive willingness to agree an offer by everybody concerned. Once the offer is agreed, the case can be tidied up and put away. Statistical reports can be completed, recording both the amount of the omitted income disclosed and the short period of time required to complete the enquiry. No one wants a case to drag on, messing up all the statistics and clogging the system. Give the Inspector a reasonable chance to agree a settlement on terms acceptable to you and you may have a pleasant surprise. If on the other hand you are greedy and obdurate, there may still be a surprise but it will be far from pleasant.

13 VAT

It must be acknowledged that if profits are understated then the VAT position will also be incorrect. There has been press publicity and comment on the arrangements made between the Inspector of Taxes branch of the Inland Revenue and the Customs and Excise concerning exchanges of information between these two branches of the Inland Revenue. Formerly all exchanges of information were prohibited and the disclosure of information from one branch to the other was considered to be inappropriate. Any officer engaged in such a disclosure would be in breach of his own departmental instructions and could be prosecuted under the provisions of Section 182 FA1989. The introduction of VAT into the taxation scene has brought a new element to the relationship between the Inspector of Taxes and the Customs and Excise. The interdependence of the accuracy of accounts for VAT, Income Tax and Corporation Tax purposes is obvious: it would, therefore, be absurd for the Customs to carry out an investigation and to obtain a pecuniary settlement in respect of understatements of VAT without passing that information on to the Inspector of Taxes, and vice versa. Nevertheless, that absurd situation was allowed to exist and, when finally addressed, was only partially remedied. Currently all exchanges of information between the Inspector of Taxes and the Customs and Excise must pass via their respective Head Offices. There is no official exchange of information permitted at grass root levels. This means that only cases reported to the respective Head Offices come within the purview of the information exchange arrangements.

The Exchange of Information
The limited information exchanges that take place do draw the attention of the 'other' branch to the larger cases that have been settled and to what has been discovered. However, the different *modus operandi* of the branches will produce quite different results from the investigations carried out. The Customs Officers, perhaps for historical reasons, generally work to prove criminal offences so that criminal prosecution standards of evidence must be achieved. This entails wide-ranging operations such as covert surveillance, painstaking physical searches of

suspect(s)/and their vehicles and belongings. Forays into the Tax Inspector's area of operation, meeting a work culture more concerned with indirect evidence and inferences based on business economics, have been reported with some derision – especially the type of investigation such as one concerned with the number of portions of peas, that should be expected from a bulk supply, and hence the turnover appropriate to the stock used. The Customs' initial enthusiasm for taking such cases before VAT tribunals has no doubt been blunted and their approach is more circumspect. The main historical thrust of the Customs and Excise is on investigations of the more robust, quasi-police variety.

Following up a Customs investigation can be quite illuminating. From the outset an Inspector is not trying to show that something is wrong: there is evidence on the table that profits have been understated and the means adopted, at least for some specific offences, have been established. However, the Inspector does not simply adopt the figure of omitted income taken by the Customs Officer in his settlement, he goes back to his traditional approach of examining the private side, looking at the taxpayer's assets, expenditure and admitted income. The outcome is normally a settlement involving a considerably larger sum for the understatement of profit and over a longer period than that negotiated by the Customs Officer.

The Customs investigation is, by its very nature, restricted to current business records that are available for inspection. He carries out test purchases and then seeks to show that the sale has not passed through the books and records of the business. Alternatively he will have other direct evidence of the commission of an offence – evidence that can be produced in court to sustain a prosecution. It is in the face of such evidence that the taxpayer makes his offer of a pecuniary settlement rather than face prosecution.

You cannot assume that because you have had a settlement with the Customs regarding VAT offences, the Inspector has knowledge of those offences; neither should you take for granted that because you have had an Income or Corporation Tax settlement, the Customs have been informed of that settlement. On the other hand, if you are prosecuted by one or other of the Inland Revenue branches, liaison at Head Office – quite apart from normal press publicity – means that the circumstances of your case will be well known to both branches. However, even in these circumstances *you* would be expected to initiate a disclosure to the branch of the Revenue not concerned with the immediate prosecution proceedings.

Anyone who has admitted substantial understatements of income for Income or Corporation Tax purposes should take steps to have the corresponding VAT position corrected and, indeed, to have the VAT element correctly dealt with in any settlement with the Inspector. After all, you will be assumed to have taken VAT into account when agreeing your figures with the Inspector of Taxes, so that the agreed omissions are all net of VAT. This aspect tends to be neglected or overlooked.

If a VAT settlement is negotiated payment of the additional VAT will necessitate a revision of the business accounts. As part of his professional duties, your accountant will ensure that such an adjustment is made and appears on the face of the accounts. You may anticipate that the Inspector, on seeing such an entry will be more than a little curious about its origin. It is, therefore, better at this point to accept whole-heartedly that confession is good for the soul – if not for the bank balance – and get the whole wretched mess cleared up as expeditiously as possible.

Customs *v* HM Inspectors of Taxes

There, is a peculiar dichotomy between what is morally correct and what is law, a division which appears unnatural and unacceptable to many people. If the powers that be can establish a legal claim on you by raising legally valid assessments or charges on you, then clearly you have to pay the tax involved. If, however, the law applicable to the different imposts involved is itself different, requiring varying levels of proof, then you may have divergent results in respect of the same source.

The Customs and Excise, as has been said, tend to collect direct evidence of an offence and do not normally proceed on the basis of inference. Therefore, they generally do not look at the accretion of the private wealth of the taxpayer and ask how he was able to acquire it, in the face of his known outgoings and absurdly low income. The Inspector of Taxes, on the other hand, will think of hardly anything else. The result is two quite irreconcilable sets of figures which will be adopted for settling different taxes actually based on the same root figures – the turnover and expenditure of the business concerned.

It is in just such circumstances that the form of the taxpayer's disclosure is so important. If the taxpayer has confessed in some detail how extractions have been made, and the amounts involved, there is really no defence against the VAT claims that flow from the figures. It would also be quite *indefensible* for the taxpayer to fail to draw the additional VAT liability to the attention of the Customs and Excise. A different position exists if a taxpayer, while making no admissions, tacitly accepts that the Inspector could raise additional assessments on him which he would not be able to prove excessive. The taxpayer's acceptance of the position here is as much a pragmatic acceptance of the way in which the legislation has been formulated as anything else, and does *not* amount to the specific admission of the actual execution of an offence.

Each branch will seek to establish its own case, from its own evidence. However, it may mean that statements made by you to the Customs Officers are made available to the Inspector. The Inspector will put the statements to you at an interview for your comments, and also to verify that they were made by you and carry your signature. In this way the Inspector can add the statements to his own documents for submission to the Commissioners and so on as evidence in support of his case.

Some Inspectors in specialist branches of the Inspectors' branch may adopt similar surveillance activities to those adopted by Customs Officers. They may be concerned with identifying persons using a variety of names where, for instance, photographic evidence may have to be coupled with the statements of witnesses to establish the relevant facts. Such procedures are, however, relatively restricted in application.

The police, naturally, are interested in information that may be in Revenue files, however, all Revenue staff have strict instructions not to divulge any information to persons not *specifically authorised* to receive it by the taxpayer. It has been made abundantly clear to staff that any breach of Section 182 FA1989 will be severely dealt with by the Board. The police are similarly unwilling to assist the Revenue in its enquiries, even if a particular incident has been reported in the local and/or national press.

Illegal Activities
Very strange situations may arise, such as where a person desires to set up in business with capital accumulated from the proceeds of crime and wishes to ensure that the Inspector will not allege, in due course, that the 'start-up' funds were derived from trading activities. In such circumstances it is up to the taxpayer to satisfy the Inspector that the monies did not come from earlier activities that could be chargeable to tax, and that the taxpayer had actually been involved in the commission of the alleged offences. If the offences were reported in the press, then obviously anybody could claim to have taken part and benefited from the crimes involved. A criminal record may be of assistance to the taxpayer here, perhaps evidenced by periods of absence from the employment scene while detained in one of HM Prisons. Whether the taxpayer is believed by the Inspector or not, no details of his alleged criminal activities can be passed on to the police because of the Section 182 FA1989 bar. To digress slightly, it is as well to bear in mind that there is no bar to the Revenue assessing the profits from illegal activities. The Courts have held that the Crown is not being a party to the illegal activity simply by assessing any profits made. The Taxes Acts require

that the profits of each taxable activity or source specified shall be assessed to tax and that the Crown is not a party to the activity merely by taking note that it is being carried on and has given rise to chargeable income. In practice, professional burglars are not assessed as such by the Revenue.

Confidential Documents
The Revenue will also decline the use of its papers for the purposes of third party action in the Courts. If the Inspector is issued with a writ to attend the Court with his file, he will naturally be obliged to carry out the order of the Court. It is, however, the Board's practice to instruct its officers to claim Crown privilege when called upon to produce their papers. So, although the papers are physically present in the Court, they are in a sealed parcel that is not allowed to be opened – and its contents remain unseen. The practice of the Board is to maintain each taxpayer's *strict* privacy with regard to information disclosed in connection with their taxation affairs. There are, therefore, no grounds for claiming that certain information relevant to a taxpayer's tax affairs has not been disclosed for fear of that information falling into other people's hands. Any taxpayer may rest absolutely assured that their trust will not be betrayed. The Inspector's staff only receive information on a 'need to know' basis and all of them are covered by the Section 182 FA1989 restriction.

14 Prosecutions

Special considerations apply when the taxpayer knows, at the outset, that his profits are substantially understated and that there is no way he can hope to defend the accuracy of his accounts. This situation may arise when the taxpayer is so contemptuous of the law in general, and the taxation authorities in particular, that he has thrown caution to the wind and blatantly extracted large sums for his personal use completely by-passing the business records – or worse still, passing the money through the business records and then using fabricated documentation to cover the extraction. To compound this folly, the loot may be clearly visible by the way in which it has been employed or utilised. The chances are, in such a case, that when the Inspector sends his initial letter he is already sure that there are substantial amounts to be explained and that plausible explanations are beyond anybody's ingenuity. He may already hold specific information and/or evidence concerning the offences involved. In such a case the Inspector may be considering opening the interview using the Hansard extract (see Chapter 2), with the possibility of sending the case on to the Enquiry Branch if it develops as anticipated. Such cases divide between those where serious fraud is alleged to have been committed, as defined in Section 146 FA1989 and incorporated in Section 20(c) para. 1A TMA1970 as follows:

(1A) Without prejudice to the generality of the concept of serious fraud:
(a) any offence which involves fraud is for the purposes of this section an offence involving serious fraud if its commission had led, or is intended or likely to lead, either to substantial financial gain to any person or to serious prejudice to the proper assessment or collection of tax; and
(b) an offence which, if considered alone, would not be regarded as involving serious fraud may nevertheless be so regarded if there is reasonable ground for suspecting that it forms part of a course of conduct which is, or but for its detection would be, likely to result in serious prejudice to the proper assessment or collection of tax.

134

and those cases where the offences may be the same, but where there is sufficient evidence available to mount a criminal prosecution – and because of that the offences take on a new dimension.

Potential Prosecution Cases
Cases are more likely to be worked for prosecution if they involve the fabrication of false documentation or a conspiracy to defraud the Revenue, regardless of the amounts involved, provided that the evidence to mount such a prosecution is still available. Such cases are unlikely to be worked in the District, unless the Enquiry Branch considered that the necessary evidence was probably beyond reach, in which case the matter would be dealt with by the District Inspector (or his fully trained assistant).

The taxpayer will be faced with some difficult decisions, but clearly the earlier and more 'voluntary' the disclosure to the Revenue the better. The purchase of tax reserve certificates will avoid interest running on the accumulated unpaid tax after the purchase of the certificates, at least up to the amount purchased.

The enquiry will run on standard lines, but in the more serious cases where there may be some doubts in the Inspector's mind regarding the adequacy of any disclosures made, the Inspector may ask for letters of authority from the taxpayer to approach banks, building societies, etc. and possibly suppliers and/or customers, in order to verify various transactions and the accuracy of your disclosure statements. It does considerable damage to the taxpayer's case if, after allegedly making a full disclosure, the Inspector digs up further bank accounts and additional omitted profits. If the case is really serious, the taxpayer is better employing a specialist firm at the outset rather than muddying the waters still further by having a perhaps incomplete, or misleading report of his affairs drawn up by his existing accountant – and worse still adopting the incorrect report due to his own inattention to its accuracy.

The Formal Warning
If a case is being worked for prosecution, the evidence will have to be put to the taxpayer after the formal warning in accordance with the Judges' Rules has been administered. The warning given is the well known 'what you say will be taken down in writing, and may be given in evidence'. This procedure may seem somewhat out of place to a taxpayer, but it should indicate to him that he is heading into *serious* trouble. In many cases the full import of the warning is not appreciated and may well be ignored: you should know that the Inspector is being deadly serious. Potential prosecution cases involve an inordinate amount of work by the investigator. There are normally a considerable number

of exhibits to be assembled, each item and entry being looked at by the taxpayer, and perhaps other 'interested parties', and identified as being known to them. The part played by the documentation has to be explored at length to ensure that there is no element of doubt about what is being said, or what occurred. The person who brought the document into being has to be established, together with who knew what, and when. Questions must be very simple and direct, and totally unambiguous. If a number of persons are involved, each will be seen separately, but each must be given the opportunity to comment on any testimony by another affecting their position in the case and their possible degree of culpability.

The Inspector will have drawn up a draft brief of written questions to enable him to assemble the replies given in a logical and helpful manner – helpful to the Revenue's Solicitors Branch, that is, so that they can make a recommendation on whether or not there is sufficient evidence to mount a prosecution. So each transaction and each step of each transaction will be explored in depth. Each step in the alleged conspiracy or fraud must be established by evidence and, if any link in the chain is missing, the outcome of any prosecution could be in the balance. The Board would not mount a prosecution that its Solicitors' Branch considered unlikely to succeed.

The number of steps to be taken in a complete transaction can be surprisingly large. If we are dealing, for instance, with an invoice that is wholly or partly false, you may be concerned with the order for the goods, the delivery note and the payment made to settle the account. The bank account into which the payment for the goods (in settlement of the invoice) is made will have to be examined, followed by the means used to refund the relevant part or whole of the money to the main beneficiary of the fraud. If there are others sharing in the benefit from the transaction, apart from the person supplying the false invoice, those sharing in the transaction will have to be seen, and the monies traced through their bank accounts, and so on.

In the case where a supplier is providing false invoices in respect of fictitious purchases by the taxpayer, and the taxpayer pays the 'supplier' by cheque, and then has the money returned to him by the 'supplier' less a 'service' charge, the questions in respect of one transaction could include fairly basic enquiries such as:

- Did you appreciate at the time that by claiming £X in respect of invoice number Y dated Z, that the purchases in your business records and accounts would be overstated by £X?
- Did you appreciate at the time that by inflating your purchases for the year ended 1989 by the inclusion of the false invoice number

Y, for £X, that the profits of your business for the year ended 1989 would be understated by £X?

- Did you appreciate at the time that the entries made in your books and records in respect of the false invoice number Y would mislead your accountant into including the false purchase in the total of the purchases charged in your accounts for the year ended 1989?
- Has the inclusion of the false invoice number Y actually led to incorrect accounts being produced for the year ended 1989?
- Did you know at the time of your approval of your accounts for the year ended 1989, that they are incorrect?
- Were the incorrect accounts for the year ended 1989 submitted to the Revenue with your consent and approval?
- Did you appreciate at the time that by submitting the incorrect accounts for the year ended 1989 to the Revenue that your tax liability would be lower than it would have been had the correct figures been submitted?
- Was the purpose of the fictitious purchase transaction supported by invoice Y the incorrect reduction of your tax liability?
- Was there any other purpose for including the false invoice Y in your books, records and accounts, apart from incorrectly reducing your tax liability?

Questions of this type may be asked after all the others necessary to establish the full details of the transactions involved, and after the relevant exhibits have been authenticated by the taxpayer. The questions are not just rubbing salt into the wounds: they are necessary to establish beyond all reasonable doubt that you are guilty of the specific criminal offences with which you may be subsequently charged. What, for instance, if a director of a company had obtained false purchase invoices and passed them through the company's business records. The case is 'fully' investigated and the evidence assembled. In Court the man explains, for the first time, that he did not pass the false invoice through the company records to defraud the Revenue, but to defraud his co-directors and shareholders. It may be that the company, or one of its major shareholders owed him money, and the only way he could get repayment was by putting through false invoices. He may claim that the idea of the tax implications had never crossed his mind. A similar situation may arise if company sales are diverted by a director who had only a nominal shareholding in the company. He could claim that he was stealing from the company, and not defrauding the Revenue. Indeed, employees' defalcations may be admissible deductions in computing company profits.

It is to avoid the unexpected that all aspects of a transaction, the reasons for it, who benefited, and so on, are covered at the interviews. The questions are endless and go into apparently mindless, minute detail. However, the purpose is to make a guilty plea inevitable in the event of a Revenue prosecution. As an extreme example, I am aware of cases where an investigator has spent three days with one individual, going through the various exhibits and questions involved.

The Criminal Charges
The charges which may be laid at the conclusion of an investigation obviously depend on the nature and extent of the offences involved. Over the years Revenue prosecutions have involved the following charges:

- Charges under the Perjury Act concerned with making false declarations of income, etc.
- Common Law misdemeanour concerning the delivery of false accounts to the Revenue or false certificate of disclosure in connection with an investigation case.
- Forgery charges in respect of false documents.
- Charges of false accounting dealt with under the Theft Act.
- Charges of being a common law cheat involving false income tax returns and false certificates of disclosure.
- Fraudulent claims to allowances.
- Conspiracy to cheat the Inland Revenue.

The list is not exhaustive, but the more recent cases receiving national press coverage have been concerned with charges of common law cheating and false accounting.

The taxpayer's voyage of discovery through the taxation investigation processes can be quite varied, depending on the type of transactions involved and the evidence available to support them. Some taxpayers end up being prosecuted because, when challenged in the local district, they have not made a full disclosure to the Revenue. They have, perhaps, denied major irregularities and convinced the hard-pressed local Inspector that the disclosure they have made is complete and accurate. They will then have been asked to complete a formal certificate of disclosure, confirming that all the facts bearing on their tax affairs have been correctly declared, and that their assets at a particular date consist of: _____ and then follows a list of the assets concerned. If at a later date it is discovered that the certificate of disclosure is false, they could leave themselves open to a criminal charge. Often as not, however, all that it leads to is another, yet more *vigorous* investigation, and another monetary settlement, with yet another certificate of disclosure. If the latest certificate of disclosure turns out to be incorrect, you could stand quite a good chance of being prosecuted – after yet another expensive Revenue investigation.

The Selection of Prosecution Cases
Persistent offenders in evading tax are not encouraged by the Revenue, and you may well find the specialist investigators from the Enquiry Branch going through your affairs with a fine toothcomb. If the persistent offences are sufficiently heinous to warrant Enquiry Branch attention from the outset, or after preliminary investigation in the local district, you could find yourself faced with criminal charges. There is, however, a limit to the number of complex criminal fraud cases that the Solicitors' Branch is capable of handling, so investigators may not do the necessary digging to find the evidence necessary to support a criminal charge. They may content themselves with establishing the full extent of the monetary loss to the Revenue, rather than seeking all the documents relating to the mechanics of the transactions involved. A lot will depend on the actual investigator working the case. Some Investigators spend the whole of their stint at Enquiry Branch without becoming involved in a single prosecution, while others may be involved in a number of cases.

Another determining factor is the nature of the taxpayer's business activities. Bookmakers for instance may feel that, dealing in a cash trade with little documentary evidence of their businesss transactions, they are in a better position than most to evade tax by understating their profits. Take for example the situation where the bookmaker puts through fictitious winning bets, with himself as the beneficiary. In normal circumstances it would be well nigh impossible to obtain the evidence necessary to sustain a criminal prosecution. It may be that a number of cases have been investigated in local districts, and substantial monetary settlements have been successfully negotiated with individual book-makers. There will, however, have been no publicity about such cases as all the proceedings before the Commissioners and all the negotiations in the Inspector's office are confidential, and cannot be disclosed to the public. Therefore, no one knows of the Revenue successes and other bookmakers may be being tempted to follow in the footsteps of those already dealt with in the local investigations. A successful prosecution of one bookmaker could, with its attendant publicity, give other potential offenders pause for thought. So if the opportunity arises to mount a prosecution in such a case, it is likely to be seized upon eagerly. On the other hand, a complex fraud case, where the outcome may not be clean-cut and the workload involved is forbidding, will not have the same attraction. Furthermore, the persons involved in the complex case may be prepared to enter into a monetary settlement that could include a penalty far in excess of anything that might be contemplated by the Courts. The temptation to charge the bookmaker, and do a deal with the fraudsters may, in such circumstances, be great – if not over-whelming.

Decisions on whether or not to prosecute are taken by the Board on the advice of the Solicitors' Branch. It is not possible for me to say, therefore, what actually transpires at such meetings. However, resources and policy must have a bearing on the outcome. If the Parliamentary Accounts Committee are pressing the Board to mount more prosecutions, to catch up with the efforts of the Department of Social Security, no doubt the Board will react as best they can with the resources at their disposal.

Gathering the Evidence

The evidence to support criminal charges is gathered in a number of different ways. The easiest is that provided by the taxpayer who, after having been given the formal warning, makes a full and frank written confession. It does not happen every day of the week! If, however, the taxpayer is vague, forgetful and confused about the details of the transactions involved, and corroborative supporting documentary evidence is not available to put to him to refresh his memory, there may be insufficient evidence to mount specific charges – and to prove them beyond all reasonable doubt. After all, if the taxpayer has been inexact in his statements, the Revenue could find when the charges are laid that the taxpayer pleads not guilty, when a guilty plea has been anticipated.

More often than not taxpayers are not co-operative in Revenue enquiries until they are advised that they are in such a fix that their best bet is to make a full and frank disclosure, pay the tax and throw themselves on the mercy of the Court. The Inspector cannot, even if the circumstances suggest that this has been done, be *sure* that a full disclosure has been made without going back to all the prime documents and evidence available to see if there are any indications of other bank accounts, etc. or further irregularities. In some instances, the taxpayer's affairs are so complex that they cannot say themselves how much has been extracted, or recall all the individual transactions involved. The Revenue investigators have to start where they can to piece all the evidence together, and to carry out such cross-checks as are considered productive and appropriate.

Using letters of authority from the taxpayer, or obtaining Section 20 orders if co-operation is limited or non-existent, the investigators will visit banks, building societies, suppliers and customers, as they think appropriate to the circumstances of the case and the information in their possession. Picking up a copy invoice from a supplier with the clear indication that all but the price is in carbon, may be significant. Here there is a clear indication of clumsy double pricing, the copy invoice carrying the top type figure that is required for the supplier's records, while the top copy of the invoice carries the top type details and a different price that is used by the customer in his books and records. Putting the invoice and its carbon copy together can start a hunt for the cheque used to settle the account, the bank account through which it passed, together with any associated trade-off transactions between the parties involved. The detailed documentation of suspect transactions needs to be filled in by looking at the Cash Book and Sales Ledger of the person supplying the invoice, and the Cash Book and Purchase Ledger of the person making the purchase. All other attendant paperwork needs to be collected.

Calls at banks may elicit information about other accounts with different banks, or branches. No stone is left unturned in a full Enquiry Branch investigation: all sources of information, both formal and informal, will be tapped to try to ensure that the investigation is thorough and complete. It is essential to impress on taxpayers that they cannot afford to take the risk of omitting to disclose any items if the investigation is being carried out by the Enquiry Branch.

The quality of the evidence available to Revenue investigators is normally of the prime documentary type. They will not have 'fly on the wall' video cameras or finger-prints from the bank notes: they do, however, have access to the Government Chemist who may carry out any tests considered necessary on a document, etc. They could say, for instance, that particular documents have been prepared on a particular typewriter, but they would not be in a position to say unequivocally that they had been typed by the same person. Signatures and handwriting may be examined and compared when necessary, and of course any results can be put to the parties concerned for their comments.

The investigators carrying out these 'on the ground' investigations will also be keeping an eye open for items that may be of interest in connection with taxpayers other than the ones being investigated. If people are circulating in a small social group, or in a particular sphere of business, it is quite possible that practices disclosed by one taxpayer may also be being carried out by associates of one kind or another. Therefore, no opportunity is lost to collect evidence and information that could be of use in other cases, cases which may not at that time have been even registered for investigation.

Clearly the taxpayer can have no direct control over the activities of the Revenue investigators. To state the obvious, however, the investigator can only find that which *is* there to be found. The existence of documentary evidence is on the physical plain, as distinct from that which lies within the knowledge and memory of individuals, knowledge which cannot be eradicated by the taxpayer, or examined by the Revenue – without the consent and co-operation of the witness concerned.

The Revenue has very wide-ranging powers to obtain particulars and documents, a fact which should not be forgotten. It is interesting to note, however, that in one recent case where the Inspector actually obtained a Commissioner's consent to issue a Section 20 notice, the notice was held to be invalid because the Inspector refused to disclose the source or nature of the information that lay behind his request for the Section 20 order. (*Regina* v. *Inland Revenue Commissioners and Another, Ex parte T.C. Coombs & Co* – judgement 26 May 1989 Court of Appeal). The disturbing aspect of this case is the failure of the Parliamentary safeguard to the public against unwarranted invasion of privacy by requiring a Commissioner to give his consent to the order. The Commissioner was required to be 'satisfied that in all the circumstances the Inspector is justified in proceeding under this section' (S.20 (7)(b) TMA1970). In this particular case the request of the Section 20 notice requiring the production of documents, produced affidavit evidence that the documents had no connection with the taxpayer under investigation and the Revenue produced no evidence to the contrary. Then, *prima facie*, the Revenue could not reasonably have formed the opinion required to justify serving the notice. The lower Court refused to grant a judicial review of the notice but the Court of Appeal allowed the appeal against that refusal.

The crux of the matter was that the Inspector claimed to have knowledge of the taxpayer's affairs from various unspecified sources which he believed to be reliable, including one which supplied information on the strict understanding that both the identity of the source and the information should not be disclosed, and that the Inspector believed the public interest required that undertaking should be adhered to. As Lord Justice Parker said:

'In the result neither the appellant or the court had any information or evidence as to the basis of the Inspector's opinion. There was nothing to show that that which prompted the request for public interest immunity was confidential information at all.'

He later went on to say:

'Here the court was faced with a blank wall which impeded the administration of Justice.'

Prosecutions

Clearly the Courts are intent on making sure that Parliamentary safeguards are effective.

The Revenue have all sorts of information being made available to them and the identity of 'reliable sources' are, naturally, going to be jealously guarded. Taxpayers should be aware that they stand in danger of being investigated because of information supplied to the Revenue from such sources.

In conclusion, it is the nature and quality of the evidence of the offence established by the Revenue, rather than the quantum of the extractions, etc. involved, that decides whether or not there is the possibility of a Revenue prosecution.

15 A Pyrrhic Victory?

You will no doubt be familiar with the facts surrounding the Revenue's prosecution of Mr Dodd – and I do not propose to go into all of the evidence and arguments adduced during the course of the trial. However, you may recall that it was alleged that jocular letters were sent to Ken Dodd from his former accountant, Mr Reginald Hunter (who subsequently admitted 12 charges of false accounting), that referred to 'the Aladdin's Cave at Knotty Ash' and added 'Long may it remain submerged in the mangrove swamps of Merseyside'. Another letter began, 'My respects to the great drum'. These 'jokes' brought about the opening of the investigation into Mr Dodd's tax affairs. Poor Mr Dodd had no control over what his accountant wrote, or the way in which he expressed himself. It was explained that 'The Aladdin's Cave at Knotty Ash' was a reference to Mr Dodd's home and its contents, which included a store of stage props and stage equipment: 'The great drum' was one of the stage props used by Mr Dodd. Yet it was from such a small beginning, arising from a misinterpretation of the accountant's words that the Revenue investigation into Mr Dodd's tax affairs was born, an investigation that eventually led to his appearance in the Liverpool Crown Court. This seems to have been the beginning of a chapter of misunderstandings, that if known about and dealt with at the time, may well have curtailed the investigation and led to quite different results.

It was reported that 'Alice-in-Wonderland' imagination was used by accountants once working for Mr Dodd to increase his annual business expenses by £37,000. It was alleged by Mr Dodd's Counsel, that either chartered accountant Mr Reginald Hunter, or members of his staff, had added vast amounts to the expenses claims of Mr Dodd. Unknown to Mr Dodd, general expenses were increased by 400 per cent from £1,000 to over £4,000, wardrobe expenses were increased by £5,000 to £7,609, and telephone and postage charges were more than doubled. In cross examination, Mr John Collier (a partner in the Liverpool branch of the accountants Grant Thornton) is reported as agreeing that his accountancy colleague had been careless, though he was unwilling to agree that the accounts proved that Mr Hunter had been clearly irresponsible or dishonest.

144

A Pyrrhic Victory?

Mr Dodd is reported to have told the jury at his trial that he kept £336,000 in cash at home rather than in the bank, to prove to himself that he was a star. He told the jury that the money represented his savings; his wages for 40 years of hard work. He is reported as saying, 'I am an honest man and I realized I had made a mistake. I had done nothing dishonest; mistaken maybe, but not dishonest.'

The Revenue alleged that Mr Dodd had deposited £700,000 in cash in banks in Jersey and the Isle of Man, without declaring a penny of interest. It was said in Court that 'He kept silent, not only to the Inland Revenue but also to his accountants trying to put things right'. Mr Dodd had explained that he had read articles and seen advertisements that had convinced him that money invested in the Isle of Man was tax-free, and outside UK tax laws. The advertisements, since outlawed in the UK, were described in Court by an accountant as 'potentially misleading'.

Mr Dodd is reported to have told the Court that he had not declared his overseas savings as part of his assets because he believed it had nothing to do with the Inland Revenue. He is further reported to have said, 'I thought they were being nosey'.

Mr Dodd's Counsel drew attention to the prosecution's failure to call as a witness Mr Reg Hunter, Mr Dodd's accountant from 1972 to 1982, who was the man who might have helped to throw light on the case. It was suggested that was because he might put at risk a prosecution where the stakes were high: 'It is a disgraceful avoidance of the truth'.

Mr Hunter had pleaded guilty to eleven charges of false accounting at Mold Crown Court, North Wales, but the 'disgraceful way' he kept the accounts was the reason Mr Dodd was now in a mess, it was claimed by Mr Dodd's Counsel.

Evidence was given of Mr Dodd's work for charities over the years, and of the large sums he had raised for them. The judge told the jury that Mr Dodd's good character was relevant to the case. The judge also invited the jury to give 'appropriate weight' to the strong criticism made of the prosecution by the defence Counsel for failing to call Mr Hunter to give evidence.

Mr Dodd was found not guilty by unanimous verdict on four charges of false accounting and one of intent to defraud, leaving three fraud charges on which the judge accepted a majority not guilty verdict.

It is said that Mr Dodd had already paid £450,000 in owed tax, and had lodged a further £375,000 with the authorities in tax certificates and bonds against a tax bill which was believed to be around £825,000. The Revenue refused to comment on the possibility that civil penalties would be sought. The defence is estimated to have cost in the region of £300,000 in legal and accountancy fees.

'It was agreed by the defence that the Revenue acted responsibly in bringing a prosecution. There was never any issue about the certificates being incomplete or incorrect. The issue for the jury concerned Mr Dodd's honesty and it is upon that issue they have returned their verdict.'

Counsel for the Revenue indicated during the course of the trial that if Mr Dodd had confessed to all previous undeclared income, it was unlikely that any criminal action would have been taken against him. Mr Dodd, however, had explained in evidence that 'I said there is nothing wrong with my accounts, nothing wrong at all. They said it was a chance to come clean, but before coming clean you have to do something wrong and I didn't know I had done anything wrong'.

While this case is unique, there are universal lessons to be learned. The first is that *nobody* should leave their taxation affairs to an accountant without taking a close personal interest in what is being done in their name. The second point is that, once a Revenue investigation is opened, you should (in serious cases) take independent legal advice regarding any shortcomings that there may have been regarding the information made available to your accountant. The third point – and probably the most unpalatable – be prepared to do a deal with the Revenue and do not stand out at all costs, just to clear your name in their eyes, by going to a Court of Law. Fourthly, appreciate that, while the Revenue may not be able to sustain a criminal charge, civil proceedings for penalties under the Taxes Acts are far more easily established. In civil proceedings the offence only has to be proved on the balance of probabilities, while a criminal charge must be proved beyond all reasonable doubt.

My advice is: if at all possible, negotiate – do not litigate.

16   An Honest Review

You will have seen from the penalty sections that the starting point for the main penalties is expressed as an amount not exceeding, and then follows details of the various amounts involved. The Inspector will be primarily interested in the amount of the tax lost due to your incorrect or late returns, etc. It is on this figure that he will base his computation of the mitigated penalties considered appropriate to your case. For 1988/9 onwards the penalty for failing to give notice of chargeability to income tax was increased to a penalty not exceeding the amount of the tax for which he is liable, in respect of income from that source for that year, under assessments made more than twelve months after the end of that year. Prior to FA1988, the maximum penalty for failing to give notice of chargeability was a mere £100. For cases of failure extending back beyond 1988/89 the Inspector will have to have regard to the lower maximum penalty in arriving at an appropriate mitigated penalty. With this one exception, the Inspector's starting point is the amount of the tax lost. In practical terms it does not matter whether the offence is fraudulent or negligent conduct; the starting point is the same, if the case is to be concluded by a monetary settlement. Once you have a fraud classification there is, however, the possibility of the taxpayer being prosecuted for the criminal offences involved.

The Board's policy for deciding which cases to prosecute obviously depends upon the quality of the evidence available, the resources at its disposal for processing the cases, and being able to get them before the Courts with the minimum of delay. The Solicitors' Branch of the Inland Revenue will advise the Board on the strengths and weaknesses of the cases submitted to it, with prosecution in mind. It is the Solicitors' Branch that is responsible for drafting the charges and for seeing the cases through the committal proceedings. The solicitors also instruct Counsel to represent the Board in the Crown Court or Central Criminal Court. The investigator is only brought in at a fairly late stage to be seen by Counsel to clear up any aspects not clearly covered by the solicitor's instructions

To Prosecute or Not to Prosecute?

Attention has been drawn to the discrepancy between the number of prosecutions mounted by the DSS and those initiated by the Board of Inland Revenue. Such comment is ill-informed and presumably stems from a basic misunderstanding of the different qualities of evidence likely to be available. DSS cases are quite cut and dried: showing that a person was in fact in employment or trading on his own account while claiming to be unemployed and drawing benefit is fairly simple. The evidence necessary to establish the case is straightforward and presents no difficulties. A similar situation arises for taxation purposes in respect of fraudulent claims for personal allowances. It is a vastly different situation when you are dealing with business receipts that are likely to have no documentation as they may well not have figured in any business or private records. There are few taxpayers so intent on being prosecuted by the Revenue that they fully document the omitted transactions and then preserve all the necessary documentary evidence to be discovered by or voluntarily submitted to the Revenue together with a full confession. Most taxpayers seem to feel that they will, somewhat belatedly, pay their debt to society by entering into a pecuniary settlement with the Board on a 'catch-as-catch-can' basis. Indeed, there is a well trodden path by those who have no documentary evidence of their misdeeds, a lack of comprehension as to how monies have been 'misplaced', but have a willing reluctance, in all the circumstances, to negotiate a suitable monetary settlement.

The types of offences that tend to figure in Revenue prosecutions are false accounting, common law cheat and conspiracy to cheat the Commissioners of Inland Revenue. The facts behind the charges are concerned with the submission of false statements of assets, false income tax returns, false certificates of full disclosure in investigation cases, and false accounts in support of income tax returns. If you are a solicitor, an accountant, or employed in connection with the administration of the law (e.g. as a barrister, General Commissioner, Clerk to the Commissioners, etc.), you are both more likely and less likely to be prosecuted. You are more likely to be prosecuted because the Board take a very serious view of such persons being engaged in fraud, but less likely to be prosecuted because your knowledge of the law is likely to keep you out of harm's way.

Fraud has been described in Halsbury's *Laws of England* as '. . . any misrepresentation made without an actual and honest belief in its truth is fraudulent'. Therefore, to show fraud it is necessary that the statement is a misrepresentation, that it is untrue, and that the person making the statement must have either *known* it was untrue or made it recklessly, without caring whether it was true or not. Couple this with the fact that

148

the charge must be proved beyond reasonable doubt for criminal standards and you will appreciate the degree of co-operation normally required from the taxpayer to place the noose around his neck.

The Moral Position

Morally and socially, burglary, theft and fraudulent activities are quite unacceptable. Offences concerned with taxation appear to be generally more acceptable to society, being associated with petty smuggling of the type in which persons returning from holiday sometimes engage. There is a quite misplaced sympathy for the perpetrators of Revenue offences although the offences are against the general tax-paying population rather than against an individual. Nobody appears to be prepared to educate the great British public in this matter, as the political establishment of all shades of opinion try to distance themselves as far as possible from the revenue raising activities in which they all engage when in office.

In the collection of taxes, it is the taxman who is held responsible, not the Government. If on the other hand there are any refunds to be distributed, it is the benign Government and not the wicked taxmen who are responsible for returning the taxpayers' money. It is a little like the drunken driver who, in the past received the benefit of every doubt from magistrates, who sometimes appeared to work on the principle of 'there but for the grace of God go I'. Fortunately education has transformed public opinion on this form of murderously anti-social behaviour, but diddling the taxman is still very much in vogue.

I recall one individual who had understated his profits over a period of years and kept the money under his carpet. His reason was that he believed he'd be a fool to return his full profits. There is indeed some truth in the belief that for the self-employed, taxation is to some extent a voluntary tax – that if the taxpayer is not greedy or inept, he may make his own decision, within reason, on the amount he choses to contribute to the Exchequer.

The Revenue, spurred on by the Parliamentary Accounts Committee, will seek to justify its expenditure in administering the taxation system. No doubt the statistics produced appear quite impressive, but they will probably conceal more than they reveal.

In my opinion standards of professional behaviour are no better than the standards of the populace at large. They improve when there is no profit in misbehaving: when the chances of detection are good and the penalties are severe. At present a good accountant can charge very substantial fees and have more business than he can cope with. In this context, a good accountant tends to be defined as one who can cover his fees by the amount that he 'saves' in taxation. Such savings are, of course, unlikely to be available to be made year in and year out. Accountants may, in these circumstances, be prepared to not seek instructions to do more than prepare accounts from the books, records and information supplied. It is then left to the Revenue to initiate any critical review of the accounts, and the records on which they are based. The outcome appears to be that we tend to have amateur tax evaders with, perhaps, inappropriate professional assistance. When the whistle is blown, everybody seeks cover.

Specialist Advice

It is not uncommon for specialist advisers who are brought into a Revenue investigation to be horrified by what has transpired prior to their appearance on the scene. Taxpayers make a habit of being wise after the event, and I must say I can sympathize with the specialists who despair at the way in which the taxpayer's case has been allowed to be presented. Their one universal wish is that they could go back to the beginning and start again: many taxpayers share these feelings. There is, however, no going back. You must get it right the first time around, and to do that you need to be personally well-informed concerning the Revenue investigation procedures and to have sound, *effective* professional advice.

Cases can progress – if that is the right word – with the original accountant passing the enquiry over to a specialist, who having produced a series of detailed but conflicting capital, income and expenditure statements that are rejected by the Inspector, advises the taxpayer to go to a solicitor to instruct Counsel. In due course interviews are held with the Inspector at which the taxpayer's two accountants, his solicitor and Counsel are all present to discuss a means of settling the case. The cost is appalling and a complete waste of money, not because the people involved are incapable of settling the case, but simply because no one told the taxpayer in words of one syllable that all the professional advisers in the world cannot put the clock back and save him from the consequences of his own greed and stupidity. They could all do a wonderful job if starting from a different point from the one established by the taxpayer and exacerbated by changing professional advisers at the wrong time. You are, without doubt, best served by one good professional accountant, keeping the heavy costs of a Revenue enquiry to a minimum, and using the professional fees saved to help fund the almost inevitable settlement.

Taking Stock

The way in which to proceed depends on a number of factors, including personal choice. A dispassionate review of the evidence which has emerged during the course of the enquiry, or is likely to emerge, is very important. But let us start at the beginning and have a stock take. Consider the following:

- Have you in fact had your hand in the till?
- Have you make a mess of your book-keeping and been slack in your overall control of the business so that business and private transactions have become blurred? Have you perhaps slipped through private expenditure invoices as business expenses?
- Have you been perhaps too trusting of your wife or partner, or have they been too trusting of you?
- What amounts have you taken, how have you utilised those amounts, and what period is involved?
- Can you recall what made you commence to extract monies and has the enquiry actually made you stop, or are you carrying on making extractions for fear that stopping will give the game away?
- How have you gone about making extractions? Did it involve falsifying business books, records or invoices, or perhaps even the forgery of invoices in support of fictitious purchases? Does the evidence still exist? If so, where is it and who else knows about it?
- Is there any direct evidence of your extractions either within your own records or anybody else's?
- Do the extractions show either directly or indirectly in your personal records, i.e. have you banked, saved or invested the money or have you spent it on normal living expenses, on the purchase of a particular asset or assets, or has it been used in a mixture of those ways?
- What amounts of extractions may be established and/or are alleged by the Inspector to have been taken from the business, and how strong is his supporting evidence? Is it direct evidence, i.e. monies from sources that cannot be explained, either lodged in bank, savings or building society accounts, or utilised to purchase assets? Is it more circumstantial, such as apparently inadequate or in-appropriately small amounts to meet your private expenditure?
- Are you going to co-operate with the Revenue in their enquiries or are you going to seek to frustrate them?
- Are you going to make a full and frank confession?
- Are you going to supply the Revenue with all the incriminating evidence that exists, including false documentation, perhaps putting the Revenue into a position where they can hardly decline to prosecute you?
- Are you perhaps absolutely innocent of having committed any breach of the provisions of the Taxes Acts?

How do you feel now?

The Best Approach

No matter what has actually transpired I think that everyone – from the extremely guilty to the absolutely innocent – will wish to bring the Revenue enquiry to a speedy conclusion, as cheaply as possible. The most expensive enquiry, in relative terms, invariably gets off to a bad start with perhaps poor or inappropriate professional advice based on half truths or downright lies from the taxpayer. The best approach is to bite the bullet and accept that you must give your taxation affairs top priority – above *everything* else. The more you do yourself, the lower the professional fees you will have to pay and the better grip you will have on what is going on between the Inspector and your accountant.

If you know that your affairs warrant a close inspection, it is better that the work is carried out by your accountant. You may concentrate on the aspects specified by the Inspector as the cause of his dissatisfaction. If your accountant is not up to the job of reviewing your affairs he will let you down, so check up yourself on his schedules. You know what assets you have and can list them. You will also know when they were acquired and from what sources they were purchased. In the first instance, the Inspector will be looking at one year's accounts and/or income tax return. This is an oversimplification, since the Inspector will have looked at a number of years; however, if the assessments have been made and any appeals for those years finalised, he may only re-open the earlier years if he can make a 'discovery'. The relevant section is Section 29(3) TMA1970 which states:

> 'If an Inspector or the Board discover:
> (a) that any profits which ought to have been assessed to tax have not been assessed, or
> (b) that an assessment to tax is or has become insufficient, or
> (c) that any relief which has been given is or has become excessive, the inspector or, as the case may be, the Board may make an assessment in the amount, or the further amount, which ought in his opinion to be charged.'

If an appeal has been made against the first assessment made on the source in question, and that appeal has either been settled by agreement or by the determination of the Commissioners, Section 54 TMA1970 provides that the assessment shall be final and conclusive. Therefore, no further adjustment of the assessment may be legally made unless the Inspector makes a discovery within Section 29.

The Courts have looked at this question of what may constitute a discovery within the meaning of the Act. The position that has emerged from a series of judgements is far from clear but, basically, the Inspector must find or discover some fresh facts that were not available to him at the time when the assessment was agreed or determined. It is, therefore, most important that any errors in the current business accounts under enquiry are shown to be exceptional and peculiar to those particular accounts and have no relevance to other years. You are, strictly speaking, in a stronger position if earlier years' assessments have been made and appealed against, rather than just having had assessments made in agreed figures without any appeals being necessary. The Board, however, knowing that accountants would seek to protect their clients' interests by ensuring that their clients' first assessments would be appealed against each year, and the appeals settled by agreement, decided to extend the same advantages to taxpayers who submitted their accounts in good time and had the agreed figure assessed in the first instance. Inspectors have been instructed to proceed accordingly, so they are bound by the same necessity to make a discovery before being able to go ahead and make additional assessments.

The initial steps, therefore, must be concentrated on establishing beyond all doubt that the current accounts under enquiry are correct, or if incorrect or defective, are only incorrect or defective in minor respects due to circumstances peculiar to that year. If the enquiry is going back into earlier years, it is up to you to ensure that the Inspector has all the necessary information to enable him to be satisfied as to the true level of profits involved and the period throughout which the accounts have been incorrect. Co-operation, in my view, should not entail attending the Inspector's office for an interview because of the heavy costs involved and the other matters already discussed. Start by ensuring that you have a first class adviser and that you are able to satisfy him of the accuracy of any proposed disclosure. If you hold anything back from your accountant, he cannot be expected to produce a full and correct report for you to adopt. It cannot be emphasied too strongly that the report to be submitted must be wholeheartedly adopted by you as your report – so make sure it is correct.

17 Conclusion

I have reviewed the various courses an investigation by the Inland Revenue may take and trust that I have made it abundantly clear that I do not believe in fighting lost causes. My view is that you should take life and the law as it is, and not try to change it. The Taxation Acts are a minefield for the unwary and it is only common sense to seek out the best professional advice that your circumstances warrant. If you are unhappy with your professional adviser change sooner rather than later: do not wait until you are embroiled in some *contretemps* with the Inspector. You should gently disengage, quietly assembling all your business books and documents in your own hands, and paying any outstanding fees.

Choosing Your Adviser
Difficulties may arise in finding the best adviser for you. Personal recommendation by someone whose judgement you trust is a good starting point, but this should be backed up by the professional qualifications of the individual or firm involved. I would personally favour a firm of chartered accountants who have a known track record and some standing in the area, but even then I would not *assume* that everything will be satisfactory. Staff may change, and personal stress and illness can lead to deteriorating levels of performance from any firm. Only accept the highest levels of efficiency and service – as the fees will no doubt warrant. When you have to make suggestions to your accountant regarding the most tax advantageous way of proceeding, it is time to be looking elsewhere. As a quid pro quo, keep your own records in immaculate order. It will save time and money in the long run, and is really just a matter of discipline and good habits. After all, you would feel more than a little foolish if a Revenue enquiry got off the ground because of a genuine mistake! The larger international or national firms may be a bit pricey but they have very good back-up facilities and are normally well-informed: they are a good safe bet.

Taxpayers often suffer ill health when they are involved in a Revenue investigation, presumably because they are aware at the outset of what

154

Conclusion

may come to light. The strain tends to build up over the years – and believe me if you string the enquiry out, it may take years to complete it. During that time you will find that there is a constant drain on your resources. Your business and family life may well suffer from the stress imposed by the investigation, with its protracted and uncertain outcome. In some instances, the Revenue investigation will drain the taxpayer's resources leaving him more or less destitute – some taxpayers have been bankrupted. I do not believe that any of them have helped themselves by trying to hinder or delay the enquiry unless it was part of a scheme to realize assets and leave the UK. Some taxpayers have done just that and sought to negotiate from afar. If, however, things are not so desperate, you are better employed in co-operating with the Revenue. After all, the enquiry has got to come to an end sometime and the devils are going to have to be paid to make them go away. Therefore, my advice is, where the case warrants it, have a good thorough capital income and expenditure review carried out and submitted to the Inspector. Enter into sensible horse-trading arrangements with the Inspector to agree figures, and make a quick payment on account in respect of any tax alleged to have been lost. This procedure will stop any further interest running on the tax that is claimed to be unpaid. Having done that, you need be in no desperate rush to finalise the penalty and Section 88 interest until you are satisfied that the Inspector is being sufficiently generous on the mitigation front.

You will be made aware of the accountancy fees building up during the course of the enquiry, perhaps by requests for payments on account. Some accountants ask for substantial payments on account before being prepared to take up the cudgels on your behalf. In some instances, due to unpaid fees, taxpayers have not been represented, have neglected their affairs and have had penalties imposed by General Commissioners for failing to render returns or to comply with precepts. This is a complete waste of money so far as the taxpayer is concerned: it simply does not pay to be dilatory when it comes to your taxation affairs.

If the Inspector is Mistaken

If you are satisfied, when challenged by the Inspector, that your books and records are correct and in good order, advise the Inspector accordingly. It is then up to the Inspector to make the running. If the Inspector wants to see any records, let him have them without delay, but make it clear at the outset that you are not prepared to allow him to go on a general fishing expedition at your expense. He may have received incorrect information, in which case the quickest way to make him go away is to let him examine the area in question. It is unfortunate that the Inspector is unlikely to disclose the cause of his concern except

155

in rather vague terms. Just accept it as a fact of life that you may never discover who or what caused the enquiry. Everybody has a 'well-wisher' or two and the Revenue is often put in the position of being manipulated to settle old scores. The Inspector is aware of this and will quickly depart if there are no easy pickings.

Finally, HM Inspectors of Taxes are public servants: the Inspector will not forget that fact, and neither should you.

Index

157

Titles of related interest from Northcote House Publishers Ltd.

THE CRASH:
and the Coming Crisis

Guy Galletly

The record collapse of stockmarkets in 1987 sent shock waves through the international financial system. Are we really in for an ominous new longterm economic downwave? Booms and busts are nothing new – nor is the market's ability to signal them. Indeed, there is serious economic evidence to suggest that great cyclical booms and busts appear in 50 or 60 year waves (which is perhaps why so few people remember them). And if a new longterm Depression is beginning, history suggests there will be very little that today's politicians and bankers can do about it.

But what of the individual? What could it mean for savings and private investment, for jobs, tax and welfare benefits, for social change, for our families and children? Are those in authority telling us the whole truth? Could a new Depression actually be worse? Written by a young economist this book is for every individual with the courage and foresight to look reality in the face. It explains the steps every individual should take to protect himself against a possible financial meltdown, and considers some of the opportunities which a radically new environment may bring. We may well be witnessing history in the making.

Guy Galletly teaches Economics at Eton College and was co-author of *The Big Bang: The Financial Revolution in the City of London.*

£6.95 paperback   128 pages   07463 053435

The BIG BANG

The Financial Revolution in the City of London and What it Means for You After the Crash

Guy Galletly & Nicholas Ritchie

The City of London underwent its biggest upheaval for more than a century – one with such serious implications for the great financial institutions that it was very aptly named 'the Big Bang'. But what was the Big Bang? How did it effect not only the insiders – banks, building societies, insurance and pension firms and the markets – but the rest of us who use their services?

Fuelled by computers and tremendous international competition, the Big Bang changed the whole face of finance in Britain. Building societies are becoming more like banks, the banks are getting into insurance, investment and stockbroking, old monopolies and traditions are being shattered everywhere.

For the ordinary citizen the Big Bang has brought immense benefits, for borrowing, investment, buying property, pensions and insurance – and better service from everyone in the financial sector. But there are great risks, too, as the new conglomerates battle for a share of today's dangerously volatile markets, shaken to their foundations by the Crash of Black October 1987. Whether you work in the City or are a consumer of finance, then *you* need to read this book. The Big Bang is affecting us all.

Guy Galletly BCom(Hons)MA was educated at Edinburgh University and Kings College, London, and teaches Economics at Eton College. He is also the author of *The Crash and the Coming Crisis* (Northcote House).
Nicholas Ritchie MA(Oxon) teaches Economics at Eton College and is the author of *What Goes On In the City?* (Woodhead Faulkner).

From Reviews of the Previous Edition:
- 'A timely study . . . reveals all.' *Times Educational Supplement*.
- 'Forthright and opinionated.' *Financial Decisions*.
- 'The most easily accessible . . . each of its chapters is short, digestible and covers a lot of ground.' *The Financial Times*.

£5.95 paperback   122 pages   07463 05495

Bank Lending

A Practical Introduction

Peter Anderson

Increased high street competition and the deregulation of financial services are putting new pressures on the modern banker. Today's professional lender must not only be able to read and understand complex business accounts; he or she must appreciate less tangible but equally important aspects of a business, for example the nature of its products, markets and entrepreneur.

- What do the accounts really indicate?
- Which financial ratios are the most revealing?
- How well or otherwise is the cash flow being managed?
- Which are the main indicators of financial stability?
- When should a lender trust to instinct?
- Why should the bank take different forms of security for different forms of borrowing?

Written for both professional bankers and borrowers, this lively and informative book meets the need for a clear introduction to how banks lend, or should lend, in today's fast-changing financial environment.

Peter Anderson is an experienced bank professional, and Associate of the Chartered Institute of Banking. A past winner of the Beckett Memorial Prize, he is Senior Banking Tutor at the Training College of one of the leading clearing banks.

£8.95 paperback   144 pages   07463 03742